CENTERING

OUR HOME ON

JESUS

Seven Principles for Parenting from Jairus' Faith in Jesus

BRIAN SCHLEY

absolutelyunprofessional.com
Wadsworth, OH

To My Family:

This book isn't my project—it's our project. It is our life. Thank you for your constant encouragement as I wrote. Tiffani, thank you for giving me the time needed to bring this book to life. You are the unnamed co-author of this adventure. To my girls, thank you for your willingness to be part of this journey. Without you, there is no book. Without each one of you, this book, not to mention my own heart, would feel incomplete.

Tiffani: My best friend. My one. Your heart for our girls is a beautiful sight. Your heart for me is treasured. Your heart for others is to be replicated. I couldn't imagine this exhilarating and exhausting journey without you.

Ashley: Your grace towards us is a gift. You are resilient, compassionate, and thoughtful. Your hugs are a comfort, and your smile infectious. I'm grateful God brought me you.

Brinley: You made me a Dad—God has blessed me. You are beautiful inside and out. You love well. Your younger sisters are blessed to have you as a model to look up to.

Cambria: You, I adore. You are filled with compassion and mercy. You love wide and care deeply. What you lack in height, you make up for in strength. Be courageous.

Lily: Smiley! You are strong and sensitive. You're also bold and courageous for others in time of need. You stand for what is right. I want you on my team, whatever we are doing.

Sophie: You put a smile on my face. My heart was yours before I laid eyes on you. You're witty and fun. The world is your playground. You are kind to everyone you meet and a friend to all.

Seven Principles

Getting Started

Parenting is no joke. It is not for the weak. Think you've got life figured out? Have kids. That'll teach you. I'm convinced that it's part of God's refining process.

I long for my kids to know and love Jesus. That's my single greatest goal and prayer for my kids. Yet, I've often wrestled with how to do that. It seems like everyone has a different opinion on every aspect of parenting. Ask ten parents a single question on any given topic, and it's likely you will hear ten different answers.

I want to figure out this parenting thing, but it's not just parenting styles and opinions I have to consider. Life comes at us from every angle. It can feel like I'm running on a treadmill—I'm working hard but not getting anywhere. Everywhere we look, there is something vying for our attention. We don't even have to go looking for it. It finds us. As much as we strive to focus on Jesus, we are challenged by the pressures of this world. All sorts of good things can take time away from what's most important. Balancing careers, kids, relationships, activities—there is no shortage of demands on our time. It can certainly be overwhelming, and that's on a good day.

I know one thing: I want my parenting to be influenced by God's Word. There are nuggets of wisdom throughout Scripture that influence our parenting. Yet, I am so drawn to stories and their impact on me that I longed to be impacted by a biblical story on navigating parenthood. Then, one day several years ago, I came across a story I'd probably read dozens of times. I was drawn to a man named Jairus. His story can be found in Matthew, Mark, and Luke's Gospels (Luke 8:40-56; Matthew 9:18-26; Mark 5:21-43). He was a guy I could relate to. He was married, had a daughter, and was trying to figure out how to parent.

Marinating in the story of Jairus for a couple years, I began to allow my mind to wander and fill in some of the blanks that the Bible doesn't tell us about his life. I connected with him. I wanted to learn from him. Certainly, Jesus is the star of Jairus' story. This is God's story. Yet, this particular story is in the Bible for us to learn from today. This led me to believe there must be more I can learn from it in relation to Jairus' parenting.

Until Jairus caught my attention, like most parents, I would typically read through Scripture and pick out key parenting gems to follow. For instance, I often need to remind myself not to provoke my kids (Colossians 3:21). Out of frustration, I can easily slip into using sarcasm or pushing their buttons. Paul's note to the Colossian church is certainly a useful reminder, one I need regularly, yet I longed for overarching principles to live by, to parent by.

I found seven parenting nuggets that I gleaned from Jairus. Those seven nuggets make up the seven chapters in this book. This is not an all-inclusive parenting book but one that offers what I believe are biblical truths we can hold near and dear as we seek to put Jesus at the center of our homes.

As I noted earlier, I don't have it all figured out. It seems this topic will be a never-ending research project on my end. I will continue to study the Bible, study my kids, and talk with people about the best ways to raise my children. Yes, I'll consider those ten different opinions from ten different parents. Why? Because parenting is worth it. I didn't write this book because I have all the answers. I wrote this book in search of answers.

Prior to having kids, I had the opportunity to work with hundreds of students as a middle school counselor. But it wasn't just my time with the students that made a lasting impact on my role as a father. It was also getting to see how different families parented all those students. As you can imagine, my counseling background influences how I interact with my kids. Did I mention that I have five daughters as my test subjects? They get the best and worst of me on a daily basis. They are the reason I want to figure out this parenting thing. They are the reason I wrote this book. My school counseling days ended when God started to draw me into student ministry. I served seven years as a youth pastor, continuing my work with students and parents, only now in a vastly different context. During these years, not only working with students in the church but also raising my own daughters, it became increasingly apparent to me the weighty influence parents have on the upbringing of their children. I became increasingly aware of the ways I was shaping my kids—for the good and bad. I had a front-row seat watching families in church parent their children. Which meant that, in this never-ending research project I call parenting, I continued to learn and grow in what it means to raise children in a Jesus-centered home. And now, with the help of Jairus' story, I feel led to share some of these insights.

If you've picked up this book, it's because you want to focus on your parenting. If you're like me, you've spent years trying to figure it out and, because you're holding this book, are still trying to figure it out. It's a never-ending battle. I used to tell our firstborn that she was going through our version of parenting trial and error. The error? We thought that by having one child, we could figure out the divine mysteries of parenting and that for the next kid(s), we would have it down. The only problem was the second kid was clearly not like our firstborn, and what worked with kid #1 did not work with kid #2. Turns out, they're all trial and error.

That said, while they may be trial and error, some principles hold true no matter the unique personality God has wired each of them with. There are principles within Jairus' story that you and I, as parents, can hold onto and engage within each of our unique homes. Through this ancient story unpacked in the following seven chapters, my hope is that God will meet you where you're at and draw you into the story written for you and your family.

Like I said, I've drawn out seven principles that we're going to explore together, and there's no better place to begin than by looking into the goal of parenting. If we don't have a destination in mind, it will be awfully difficult to get there. In chapter two, we will work through becoming the parents our kids can follow. Trusting God is a big part of this process and will be discussed in chapter three before we explore being the gatekeeper for what and who comes into our kids' lives in chapter four. In chapter five, we will work through the challenges of living differently than the world may suggest, choosing to parent according to the Bible instead. In chapter six, we shift to talking about the roles we play as parents before finishing up in chapter seven with a discussion about not parenting based on fear. Rather, we can confidently embrace this challenge as we know He is by our side. I believe these seven principles will help each of us parent our children in line with a Biblical worldview while putting Jesus as Lord in the central focus of our homes.

Now, this book isn't intended to simply be head knowledge but to impact our actions as well. At the end of each chapter, I've created a list of reflection questions. Questions I've personally been challenged by one way or another along this journey. These questions provide an opportunity for individuals, couples, or groups space to think through and discuss some of the concepts from the chapter in greater detail.

We either parent on accident or we parent on purpose. I have spent enough years parenting by accident. How about you? Here and now, with Jairus' story as a backdrop, I strive to be more intentional in my parenting. I want to parent on purpose and with a purpose. In order to do that, I knew I needed to dive into Scripture and figure out how to bring Jesus into the center of my home. To parent with Him in mind.

Do you parent on accident or on purpose?

What is your purpose?

Do you have a Jesus-centered home?

I pray this book helps bring clarity to you in each of these areas. I pray it helps you parent with a biblical foundation. I pray you put Jesus at the center of your home.

1   Our Kids Are Dying

When my phone rang a second time, I knew that meant it was important. The rule my wife and I have established is that if we call once, we will leave a message, understanding that the other person is at work and currently in a meeting. If the phone immediately rings a second time, the call is important enough to pull the person from the meeting.

With the second ring came a shutter. I suspected something was not okay. I took a deep breath and answered. My fears were quickly realized. I heard what I can only explain as "bawling" coming from Tiffani. "He thinks it came back. It's not good. The cancer came back, and it moved to the other side."

Just ten months earlier, we began a journey to find the next missing piece to our family. After months of prayer, conversations, research, and a willingness and desire to walk in God's will, we believed He was leading us to send in our application to adopt a child from China. Just a few months later, we received a file with Sophie's picture in it. As much as we quickly fell in love with our little girl, we had to face the fear of reading her limited medical file. One word stood out to us—cancer.

We sought medical advice from doctors near and far. The answers we received were as vague as her medical file. The consensus was that there was not enough information to know what Sophie's health would be like when it came time to bring her home. Case studies were limited. In America, retinoblastoma is screened for at the hospital and quickly treated in infancy. Though she was only two, it was not common to see it left untreated for so long. Surgeons removed her eye, parotid gland, and a slew of lymph nodes throughout her face and neck. Chemotherapy followed for six long months. Speaking with doctors locally, we understood the possibility that radiation could be part of her continuing treatment plan, but was not scheduled to occur in China. Our best bet was to get her home as fast as possible.

We set records. From the time we applied until the time we flew to China to be with Sophie was seven months. From our agency's standpoint, our turnaround time was blazing. We expedited every aspect possible, making frequent road trips to hand deliver paperwork in order to shave days off our timeline. It was all worth it when we laid eyes on our daughter. She was sweet and, as one of the translators called her, "spicy." She clearly had the energy needed to keep up with her three sisters waiting for her back in the States.

Not long after settling in at home, we began the frequent trips to visit her doctors. One day, following a number of appointments and an MRI, my wife, Tiffani, was taking Sophie to her oncologist to get the results from her tests. It was after that meeting with the doctor that my phone rang—twice.

JAIRUS

It is every parent's worst nightmare to hear the words, "Your daughter is dying."

Jairus heard those words, and it sent him instantly into a fear-filled panic. After what he anticipated was a common cold, a few days later, devolved into a struggle to breathe. Her pale skin was clammy to the touch. What just days prior he shook off as nothing to be concerned about now left him terrified.

Rumors of the Teacher being nearby had been rumbling through his home, and he had taken notice. Jairus must have thought what any desperate parent would, "If only I can get to the Healer, He can save my daughter." Without an exact destination, he took off toward town. Traveling fast and light, I imagine the only thing he carried with him that day was hope. He had hope that he would find the Teacher and, maybe, just maybe, the Teacher would do something.

When desperation hits, we are relentless when it comes to helping our kids. When the reality hit Jairus that his daughter's illness would lead to death, he stopped at nothing to try to help her. And just as you and I would chase down every possible lead to find a cure, he ran toward the unknown with only a glimmer of hope that he would not just find Jesus but also convince Him to come back with him. Bring the Healer to his home to save his daughter.

Here's the stark reality: our kids are dying. We all understand the idea that we will die someday. Usually, someday seems far away, and we don't actually spend a lot of time thinking about it. But maybe we should. Pause for just a moment and reflect on the idea that our kids, just like us, are dying. Sobering, isn't it?

As Christians, we understand that we have an opportunity to leave this earth and enter into eternity with Jesus. When we have kids, at some point, it dawns on us that they, too, will have the opportunity to put their faith in Jesus and spend eternity with Him. Now, I understand each person has the choice whether or not to put their faith in Jesus. Of course, there are several elements at work in their faith journey, right? We, as parents, can do our part. And we trust that Jesus is at work doing His. And there are other people who can also play key roles: youth pastors, grandparents, mentors, etc. Yet, we can't simply throw our hands in the air and say, "Jesus, it's up to you. Sure hope it turns out well." He has given our kids to us within our homes and in our contexts—for a purpose. We have a role to play. A pretty big role at that. Which begs the question, "What is our goal as parents?"

OUR GOAL

Let's go back and look at how Jairus responded in his situation. This father stopped at nothing to bring Jesus into his home. He knew his only hope of saving his daughter was to get Jesus inside the walls of his house and right next to his dying girl lying helpless in her bed.

The truth is, we need to be like Jairus. To act with the same loving determination he did the moment it occurred to him that Jesus was near and capable. Our kids are dying. They need to be saved, and Jesus is the only one who can save them. Our job, as parents, is to bring Jesus into our homes so He can save our kids and bring them into an eternal relationship with Him.

That's it. That's our main goal. The reason we were blessed with kids in the first place. To put Jesus at the center of our families.

CENTERING JESUS

We want to bring Jesus home with us.

We want to center our families around Jesus.

We want Him to be the focus each and every day within our homes.

We want to make decisions based on His will for our lives.

We want to live according to His Word.

Simply put, we want to follow Him. And we want to take our kids with us as we go.

DEFINING SUCCESS

You may have heard the saying, "Do you want to get your kid into Harvard or into Heaven?" It certainly isn't an either-or proposition, but it does bring a helpful context to light. Is our primary goal for our kids to get into a top-notch college so they can get a top-notch job and make top-notch money? While that may be part of my retirement plan, I'm not sure Jesus cares about those things as much as we do.

As much as I'd like to say I don't care about my kids being successful as the world defines it, it is awfully hard not to get caught up in grades, awards and acknowledgments. We certainly don't have problems sharing pictures of "success" on social media. Yet, I'm not sure the last time I saw a picture of a child alone in her bedroom praying at night. Or, a middle schooler who left his table of friends to go sit by someone who was all alone. Yet, these actions seem more aligned with Jesus' heart. Closer to His definition of success.

Instead, what I see are pictures posted of accomplishments. I see trophies, honor rolls and badges. I see dresses, milestones and future intentions. I see things that make us, parents, feel accomplished. Whoops, did I just say that?!

Seriously, why do we post all those highlights of our kids? Reflect on that question for a bit, and you may find the answer has less to do with them and more to do with us as parents. In all the challenges that come with parenting, it seems like we need to feel some tangible sense of accomplishment or success in how we are raising these "little sinners." So, amidst the tantrums, arguments, and eye rolls, we post smiles, victories, and hugs. We feel the need to post the highlights to all who can see in order to keep up with the Jones', whoever they are, posting their own feel-good stories.

The catch is if we choose to define ourselves by worldly standards, we will compare and evaluate ourselves according to worldly measures. Comparison is the ultimate stealer of joy in this world. When we look at the outside of others' lives, like what we see on social media, we see "picture perfect" in every season and space of their lives. We compare ourselves to the seemingly perfect families all around us and we feel inferior. And how do we respond? We dive into the fruitless "perfect post" competition, desperately trying to fit in with everyone else. All the while, behind the camera, we're struggling to measure up to the standards the world has defined for us.

The good news is, despite the endless race around us, we do not need to buy into the comparison game. We do not need to measure ourselves by worldly standards. Our goal is to measure ourselves by godly standards. Our goal is to bring Jesus into our homes and shine a light on His accomplishments. His victories within our lives. His definition of success here and now.

How do we do this? How do we actually put Jesus at the center of our families?

GO OLD SCHOOL

Let's go old school for a bit, back to the Old Testament. Deuteronomy 6:4-9 is one of those go-to nuggets of wise biblical instruction showing us how to put Jesus at the center of our families. This text is an ancient, relevant reminder that we are to love God above all things.

But it doesn't stop there. It directly speaks to us parents. We are expected to teach our kids to do the same—love God above all things. The text goes on, guiding us as to where and when we are to teach them. The gist of it? Anywhere and always. Too general for you? The author goes on to specifically point out several key times and spaces: when we are at home and when we are outside of the home and on the move, when we wake up and when we go to bed, with reminders about God's love in our hands, on our walls, and everywhere in between.

Our job, as parents, is to teach our kids about the love of God wherever we go and all the time.

There are routines we can get into as families to help us foster a love of God into our kids' lives. For example, we can have devoted prayer times in the mornings, at meals, before bed or any other time that seems to work with our family schedule. They can be structured prayers, prayers led by an individual, or prayers where everyone takes a turn. The *how* details are less important than the aspect of dedicating time toward putting Jesus at the center of our families.

Our family has a few prayer routines we hold fast to. In the mornings, we pray as we drive our kids to school. Each person takes a turn, and we pray for the day and anything else on our minds and hearts. Before we sit down to eat meals together, either one person will pray, or we'll recite a family prayer together. At bedtime, we all sit around the living room while everybody takes a turn praying out loud. Now, there are times when our kids are not full-on excited to jump into a lengthy prayer. And while Tiffani and I want them to participate, on these nights, they can simply share with everyone something they are thankful for in their prayer. These carved-out times and spaces have become some of the ways we continue to build prayer into our daily lives.

Routines help us build our home life on God. They help lay a foundation. Yet, even when we desire it, bringing Him into every other moment of our lives is tricky. If we are to teach our kids to love God with all their heart, soul, and strength, then we also want to help them understand they can pray anytime throughout the day. After all, prayer is not something we do just at meals or bedtime, as if we only connect with God at appointed times, right? Parents, the best way to teach this is to model it. Which means we want to find times throughout each day like we see in the Deuteronomy passage, where we not only incorporate prayer into our family's daily walk but we have conversations that are focused on God as well.

I remember sitting at our kitchen table one morning while feeling the stress of upcoming events and close friends going through some challenging times. The weight sat particularly heavy on me that morning, so I put my head in my hands and just started to pray silently to myself. After lifting my head back up from praying, one of my daughters was standing next to me with a concerned look on her face. "Daddy, are you okay?" she asked. "Yes, sweetheart, I'm okay. There's just a lot going on right now, with me and with some people who are hurting, so I'm just praying about all of it." Had I slipped away somewhere quiet to pray, I would have missed the opportunity to share with my kids that prayer is not just a scheduled or a solitude thing, but an all-the-time and anywhere thing.

Interruptions are a blessing. As much as it bothers me to be interrupted while I'm reading my Bible in the mornings, I believe it is more than worth it to read my Bible in an open area of our house, which for me is usually our kitchen table, a high traffic area to be sure. Our faith is built on a personal relationship, yet if we're not intentional, we run the risk of keeping it too private. So much so that our kids wouldn't get to witness what a relationship with Jesus actually looks like. Ultimately, if we are going to spend time praying and talking about God throughout each day, then our kids need to see us interacting with God. And we ought to take those opportunities to share not only about our faith but about our unique faith journey.

Our kids can lead the way as well. When sirens rang out one day while we were driving, one of our girls' ears perked up. As we pulled the car over to give space to the oncoming ambulance, Sophie was curious to know what happened that would cause an ambulance to rush by. Tiffani explained to her that it could be someone hurt who needed to go to the hospital. In her wonderful, childlike faith, Sophie quickly blurted, "Well then, we should pray for them." Ever since, whenever our girls see an ambulance going by we pause to pray for the person needing help along with all those involved.

Teaching our kids about our faith can also come through conversations. Curious questions are great conversation starters. "What do you think God thinks about that?" is one of my favorites. We have many opportunities throughout our day to talk about God if we simply invite Him into the conversation. If we are driving in the car and hear something on the radio, we can simply ask our kids, "What do you think God thinks about that?" Or if we are watching TV and something with questionable content airs, we can ask our kids, "What do you think God thinks about that?" This question is simply a conversation starter to help our children develop the habit of bringing God into every aspect of their lives.

"What is God teaching you lately?" is another favorite question I like to ask, not just for kids but for all of us. Often, we can go long periods of time without putting much thought into the idea that God is constantly trying to grow us to be more like His Son. Which means, God is constantly trying to teach us something—about who we are, about who He is, about following Him.

When we ask our kids what God is teaching them, we are teaching them to be reflective in their lives. We are teaching them to consider that God is always trying to teach them something, and if they are aware of it, they are more likely to catch it. It's the same reason we want to create healthy prayer habits while also modeling prayer in real time out in the open. When conversations *about* and *with* God become normal or routine, our kids are more likely to grasp the deeper nature of their own relationship with Jesus.

TRAIN THEM

Don't we just want the magic formula to ensure our kids will be with Jesus forever? Proverbs 22:6! "Train up a child in the way he should go, even when he is old he will not depart from it." Boom! Our magic formula. Right?! The ultimate parenting nugget of wisdom. We read that verse, and it seems to provide us a guarantee. If we just train them up right—if we read them the

Bible or take them to church on Sundays—they will never depart from the Lord.

Except that's not really what it means.

This highly popular parenting verse is popular for the wrong reasons.

We want a magic formula, but a magic formula it is not. It is, however, guidance on how we should raise our kids. Train them in the way *they* should go. Our kids were knit together by God and designed for His unique purpose. Our kids are unique, which means that as parents, we study them relationally to understand what makes them tick. What are their strengths? What gifts does it seem like God has given them? God has given all of His children unique gifts to be able to build up His Kingdom. The beauty of our faith is that we are not all the same. We need one another in order to maximize our gifts. Yes, that means within the home, alongside siblings, grandparents, and close family friends. He has designed us to work together. He has designed our kids to work together with others to make an impact for eternity. When we study our kids and begin to grasp how God has wired them, we're better equipped to help train them up according to their design. We can encourage them in their spiritual gifts. Find ways for them to contribute to the world. Grow in the skills and abilities God has set them apart for. Simply put, we can train them in the way God intends for them to go.

More and more, I am amazed when I look at how different my kids are. I laugh at times, thinking, "You all live under this roof and yet are completely different." I assumed they would share more similarities than they do, considering their daily routines, shared meals, familiar settings, and a relatively equal dose of parental attention. Yet my assumptions often fail to recognize the outsized role God's hand plays in who they are. I look at Brinley and see leadership and administration. I can look at Cambria and see compassion and drive. Lily brings joy and mercy to the world. Sophie gets along with everyone and unites people. Creativity and art pour out of Ashley.

With each of my girls, I ponder, "God, what are you going to do with her?" The catch is, if I were to stop with that open-ended thought, I would miss out on the intentional journey between where they are now and where God is taking them. You see, there's a vital, reflective follow-up question I need to consider as well. A question every parent has to ask. "How will I train them to grow in the gifting God has given them?"

Recognizing how they are wired is the first step. Calling it out in them is the next step. How? We can start by encouraging our kids by letting them know the wonderful gifts we see that God has given them. Using the phrase "I notice," followed by an example of how they've used their gifting, is a great start. I can look at one of my daughters and say, "I've noticed how people tend to follow you when you are in a group." I can tell another, "I've noticed you really care about others, especially when they're not being treated fairly." Afterward, follow up with something like: "You have a gift that God has given you. He gives different abilities to each one of us. I wonder how He wants you to use that gift." Observing and calling out the good things we see in our kids doesn't take much. And in those seasons where it might be a challenge to do so, it's probably needed all the more.

Our gifts can be polarizing. The gifts God has given us can be beneficial when used correctly. However, with the same amount of zeal, they can be harmful when used incorrectly. You can already picture this, can't you? This is usually how evil villains in movies become evil villains. Brinley, one of our daughters, has leadership gifts. She can take the lead in any situation, and others will follow. She has insight and wisdom and will share it with others. When used well, Brinley can mobilize a crowd and get people moving to accomplish great things. On the flip side, I have witnessed her push the envelope toward being bossy or pushy. She can take over situations, especially at home, that are not hers to take over. She can parent her sisters when her Mom and I are in the same room. I am confident God has wired Brinley to lead. My goal as her dad is to help her grow her leadership to the point where she can harness it for God's glory and the benefit of others. But also to help her understand how leadership can go too far where people no longer want to follow.

The gifts God has given us can be used to build up His Kingdom, or they can cause harm to others when not harnessed. Leadership is certainly one of these gifts. In order to help my daughter grow, I need to continue to observe her and be in place to watch her leadership in action, ready and willing to train her in this area. I need to spend time with her. I need to be purposeful in our time together. I need to be present when we are together.

Lily has the gift of mercy. I call her my "Micah 6:8 kid." Micah 6:8 tells us we are to seek justice, love mercy, and walk humbly with God. Lily seeks justice for others when she senses things are not fair. She has a merciful heart that is deeply compassionate toward others. Tiffani can connect with this better than I can. If gifts were passed down, this one would come from her. I don't have the gift, but can spot it in her. I admire it. How can we train our kids in something we don't have? My initial reaction to most bumps and bruises is to tell my kids to "Rub a little dirt on it" or to suggest they "Suck it up, buttercup." That's not ideal. On the other hand, Lily will see her sisters hurting and compassionately ask, "How are you doing? Can I get you anything?" When I see her reaction, I notice it, and I say something. I let her know it's a good thing that she cares for others so much that she's willing to not simply feel for them but go the extra step to want to do something about their challenges. So, I want to train her in how to seek justice. I want to help her understand what her role in mercifully helping others can look like. To do this, I have to acknowledge that this verse doesn't stop at seeking justice and loving mercy. To instill in her a healthy understanding of her gifting, she has to be aware that she'll need to walk humbly with God as well. My role, if I am to train Lily in the way she should go, is to help her humbly love God and seek His heart for His people, specifically the people she is drawn toward. Because God has plans for her, I have to ask myself, "How can I train her in the way God has made her? How can I help her understand which battles are hers to fight? How can I help her compassionate heart not get trampled on by people who will take advantage of her?"

Our kids are sponges. They absorb so much of what we teach them in their formative years. As parents, we hold the uniquely divine position of being able to help them harness and grow the gifts God has given them, training them in the way He has designed them to go. Why? So that when they are old, they will live out of what we have taught them.

Part of our role as parents is to train our kids to be the men and women God intends them to be. We train them to love God and love people as Jesus modeled this for us. We train them to utilize their gifts and to use them together with others in order to build up God's Kingdom. Our goal shouldn't be to raise the children the world wants us to raise—but to raise the children God has entrusted us to raise.

CONCLUSION

"Enjoy your daughter, enjoy the time you have together." That was the doctor's response when Tiffani asked how we should proceed after receiving news that the cancer may have returned—"Enjoy the time you have together."

What do you do with that? How do you respond to that kind of news? Well, from my experience, you start by crying—a lot. Through the tears, prayer seemed to follow. I was at church when I received that call. After talking through it with my wife and gathering as much information as possible, I paced through our sanctuary. I think I would call what I did *prayer*, but to anyone who might have heard, I would have sounded like a skipping record: "Really, God? Really? Why?" Over and over, I assured Him, "This does not make sense to me." In my uttering, I asked, "Why would you have us bring home Sophie just to bury her? Why would you want her sisters to experience that?"

As I continued to pace and audibly repeat my questions to God, at some point, I felt like I gained an answer. Through tears, anger, sadness, and ultimately, silence, I received something from God. It wasn't so much an answer as it was a response. It was the response I needed at the time. After a moment, I looked to the Heavens and said, "Well, if she's going to meet Jesus, maybe it's our job to introduce her to Him first."

As Tiffani and I continued to pray for healing, we acknowledged our role in introducing Sophie to Jesus, all the while pleading to God that he would let her outlive us.

The following week, we scheduled a biopsy where they removed two more lymph nodes, testing them to determine if the cancer had returned or if the MRI results were simply irregular. In the ensuing weeks, as we waited for her biopsy and impending results, we valued our time together—as a family. We understood some things seemed to matter more than others in life—we certainly did not sweat the small things.

We took a lot of pictures.

We played a lot.

We prayed a lot.

We focused on Jesus.

We found ourselves back in the doctor's office. The same office where, only a couple weeks prior, Tiffani had heard the dreadful news from a concerned doctor that her cancer was back and believed it may have also crossed from the right half of her body to the left. There we were, watching as the doctor returned with results from the lymph nodes biopsy.

As he sat down, he shook his head in disbelief. "The lymph nodes are cancer-free. I don't get it. I don't understand, but she does not have cancer. We will continue to monitor her closely and follow up with an MRI every three months going forward."

I didn't care what we were doing going forward. All I heard was "Cancer-free!" More tears were shed. Those tears tasted different. Joy sure is sweet.

I never again want to experience having a doctor inform us that one of our daughters may have cancer. Still, I am grateful for the process God walked with us. I often go back to my conversation with Him as I paced through the sanctuary. The words I uttered are still clear in my head. "Well, if Sophie's going to meet Jesus, maybe it's our job to introduce her to Him first."

Our kids will meet Jesus. That will happen. Our job is to introduce our kids to Him before they meet Him. Yet, I don't want to stop at introducing Him to them. My hope is that they lovingly run into His arms because they know Him and love Him. We start that process by bringing Jesus into our homes. It's what Jairus did. Jairus knew Jesus was the only one who could save his daughter, so he did everything he could to introduce Him to her.

What are we willing to do to bring Jesus into our homes? What is our goal as parents? As I reflect on the weeks between that dreaded MRI and the results from the biopsy, I realize how easy it is to settle into a life where Jesus is an afterthought. During that short, painful season, we were hyper-focused on being purposeful parents, intentionally bringing Jesus into our home to resume His place as the center of our family. Now that it's been a few years, I find myself needing to remember those days. I desire to reflect on them regularly in order to grasp the purpose I want to live out as a parent. To give them over to what God has planned for their lives and usher them toward it.

How about you? What is your purpose?

1 REFLECTION QUESTIONS

1. Are you able to recall a defining moment as a reminder of God's purpose in your life? What is it about that story that still has an impact today?

2. Can you relate to Jairus? If you were in his sandals, how might that experience remind you of God's purpose for your life and home?

3. How has God designed your child(ren)? How would you complete the following sentence: When my child grows up, I want him/her to be _____.

4. What comparison traps do you tend to fall prey to? How will you overcome them? What godly standards can you rely on in place of the world's standards that ensnare you?

5. What are your current family rhythms that place Jesus at the center of your home? Are there rhythms and habits you would like to start? What are they? Be specific.

2 My Work Here is Done

I was working from my makeshift office, our kitchen table, when I heard squabbling from the bedroom. Two of my girls were arguing incessantly over trivial things—like many of their disagreements. I found myself getting annoyed. I simply wanted to be able to knock out a couple hours of work that morning, but I could not shake the distractions from my mind.

When one of my little arguers came over to complain about her sister being mean to her, I had already declared myself done with mediating another argument. I had plans to get a couple early quiet hours in, and my plans were being shifted by irrational, arguing little sinners.

Most of the time, I would hear out the complaint, talk it through, then, modeling problem-solving skills, help them navigate their response. That is not what I did. In my state of annoyance, I sarcastically responded with, "I bet if you punch her in the nose, she'll stop."

Sarcasm doesn't work in parenting.

BRIAN SCHLEY

I know sarcasm is not an effective form of parenting. I get the sense we all know this. But it felt so good to blurt it out in the moment. Knowing she would understand my sarcasm and realize their argument was over nothing, I anticipated they would go on with their day, hugging and playing joyfully.

Unfortunately, some of my kids have adopted my spiritual gift of sarcasm and can easily find the humor in my comments. This kid didn't.

About five seconds after telling her to punch her sister in the nose, I heard a cry coming from the bedroom. The formerly mean sister came down the hall crying. "What happened?" I asked. "She punched me in the nose," she yelled!

My work here is done.

I spent the next few minutes apologizing to both of them and asking for forgiveness. I apologized to the first daughter for not hearing her out, teaching her how to respond to the situation, and giving her not-so-good advice. To my daughter with the sore nose, I apologized for telling her sister to punch her instead of working their disagreement out.

Sarcasm or not, our kids are looking for guidance. Each day, we have the opportunity to teach them how to live this life. They are sponges who soak up everything we say and do. They listen. They watch. They absorb. The question is, what do our kids hear, see, and take in when they listen, watch and absorb? They look to us to figure out how to handle all that life throws at them. They follow what we do and say. They follow in our footsteps.

JAIRUS' FOOTSTEPS

Jairus' footsteps led him to Jesus. When he was in his most challenging moment—when his daughter was dying—he ran to Jesus. Yet, I don't get the impression that this was new to Jairus.

When facing hard times, we look for something that can help. We will go to people or things that have provided relief in the past. All the more, in a moment of desperation, we don't tend to reach for something new, unproven, or radical. When desperation hits, we want to go towards the people or things we can count on the most. When Jairus' daughter was dying, he ran to Jesus.

Jairus ran until he found Jesus. And when he found Him, he fell at His feet.

As a leader of the synagogue, Jairus may have heard Jesus' teachings prior. He would have heard the stories, the miracles, the rumors, the frustrations, and the animosity. He would have had a choice to make, "What do I do with Jesus? Some say He is God. Others say he is a good teacher. Some argue he is a menace to the world."

Like many others, Jairus could have denied Jesus' claims and actions. He could have chosen to maintain his reputation and ignore Jesus. Instead, Jairus' decision was to fall at Jesus' feet. He believed Jesus was who He said He was. And because of his belief, Jairus ran to Him when confronted by his greatest need. When he was desperate, when he had one shot to make it all right, Jairus ran and fell at the feet of Jesus.

This couldn't be the first time Jairus put his trust in Jesus, could it? I cannot imagine that in his crisis moment, as he wrestled with his options, he would come up with a wild-card idea to go after someone he heard some strange things about.

BRIAN SCHLEY

When I am in a bind, even something trivial at home, I call people I trust. If the heat goes out, I call the company that has done work at my home before—assuming it was done well, of course. If it's a plumbing issue, I call the plumbing company that has helped us out. If my car is acting up, I'm going to the garage I can count on. Even in these trivial matters, especially when time is of the essence, I'm not taking chances on some new person or place or crazy idea. I'm going with what I believe to be my best shot.

Jairus was going to take his best shot when his daughter's life was on the line. He was going with the person he could trust the most in this situation, believing in what Jesus had to offer. Fully trusting that Jesus was the only one who could save his daughter. So, he headed out from his home, went to find Jesus, and fell at His feet.

GOOD OR BAD

If you can't tell already, I want to be like Jairus. I want to run after Jesus. I want to fall at His feet and plead for my children.

I want to run after Jesus whether my kids are in dire need or thriving. I want to fall at his feet as a daily posture. I want my kids to follow me as I chase after Jesus rather than chase after my sarcastic comments. Like I said earlier, they will follow us—good or bad.

It is "fun" to watch all of our bad habits on display in our kids, isn't it? Like the time one of my kiddos got hurt and, whimpering, came to me for some affection. How did one of her sisters reply? "Suck it up, buttercup." "Hey!" I responded. To which the unloving sister replied, "What? It's what you always say." Oooh, dagger.

Our kids pick up on what we say and do, whether we see it or not. They are figuring out this world by watching us. It is why that passage in Deuteronomy about walking, sitting, and waking together is so relevant. The things we say, do, and value become their first thoughts and beliefs.

So, what do we value? If our kids are watching us to determine what they should value in this world, what are they seeing in us?

Now, if you're the churchy (Wisconsin) type like me, you would probably say something like, "God, family, and the Green Bay Packers!" For some of you, this list will look slightly different, though, more often than not, with the top two landing in the same slots. Let me ask you—is that actually true? Are those your stated values—you know, the ones you tell others, maybe even yourself—or do you actually live out these values? In other words, are your proclaimed values an accurate reflection of what your kids see in you? In your home?

What do we really value?

VALUES

The three C's. The C's are an easy trick to determine what we value. Looking at our calendars, cash, and conversations, we can understand what we value. This is where we move from saying what we value to seeing what we value based on how we live our lives. If we honestly take stock of how we spend our time, how we spend our money, and what we talk about, we will be able to review a more honest picture of what our current value system truly is.

Calendar

How do we spend our most valuable resource—time?

One hundred sixty-eight. It's a magic number. It's the great equalizer. It's the number of hours we get to live each week. Every person has the same number of hours each week to figure out what to do with.

To evaluate the approximate value of how we spend our time, we should look at our calendars. You can imagine that not everything we give our time to shows up on our calendars. So, we'll need to dig in a little deeper. We'll need to take some time and reflect on what we do while we are at home in order to catch a more realistic picture regarding what we value.

If you aren't sure, ask someone who spends time with you. Ask your spouse or your kids. What do they see you doing the most? What do they see you prioritize in your daily, weekly, monthly, and yearly rhythms that they might end up replicating?

Let me suggest we all eliminate a phrase that is commonly used when it comes to how we manage our time. "I'm too busy." Or any variation along those lines. The thing about this phrase is that it has become a casual excuse for not wanting to do something or for not wanting to think through our priorities.

Instead of saying, "I don't have time for_____," let's be honest with ourselves and others and try saying, "That just isn't a priority for me right now." It may seem like a drastic change or a curt statement, but I have found it to be an earnest one. When approached with a request that would normally warrant the reply, "I'm just too busy," again, if we're being honest with ourselves, we can simply admit that whatever it is doesn't rise up to the level of importance necessary to make it onto our calendar. For example, if someone asks you to cancel your plans for the next day to help them weed their huge garden (assuming you're not into weeding large gardens), you would typically let them know that you would love to, the problem is, you are just too busy. Yet, suppose someone were to suggest you clear the next day's schedule to be treated to a spa day, get backstage passes to your favorite band, or sit in box seats at your favorite team's game. In that case, you may suddenly, if not miraculously, be free.

When my wife was pregnant with our first baby, we talked about taking a vacation soon in order to get the nursery ready and be fully prepared for her arrival. The way a responsible, first-time dad would. We talked as we went to bed that night about scheduling it a week away, as she was only thirty-seven weeks along at that point. Obviously, we had plenty of time. The next morning, I woke up to my wife rubbing my shoulder and asking if I could call off work that day. As I wiped the sleep out of my eyes, I answered, "Hun, we talked about it. Today, my schedule is jam-packed. I can take off next week so we can get ready." To which she gently replied, "My water broke." "Yup! I'll call in!" I yelled as I jumped out of bed. Suddenly, my priorities shifted. I went from, "Sorry, I'm too busy today," to "Yes, I can absolutely do that." The shift was not related to the busyness on my calendar. The shift sprang from priority.

Now, I am a fan of the principle that we should honor our first "yes." This means that if we commit to something, then we should honor that commitment. I stand by that. For the most part. So I'm not suggesting that we just go through life taking the best thing that comes while bumping whoever or whatever was on our schedule previously. That would not only be unproductive but a rather dishonorable way to make decisions.

So, what should we do? How can we establish and maintain a

healthy work-life balance? How do we discern when to honor a commitment and when to honor a priority?

Establish our priorities. Name our priorities. Schedule around priorities. When we name what we want to be about, then we can schedule around our priorities first and foremost. Whatever else comes at us gets filtered through our priorities before hitting the calendar.

If God is a priority, then schedule Him in. That can mean Sunday services are non-negotiables. Or that volunteering at church or in the community is scheduled as a priority. It might mean that a Bible reading plan or prayer time is scheduled and held firmly in place when something else comes up. We schedule around our priorities, not the other way around. It is easy to say God is a priority in our lives. Lots of people say it. But unless we schedule Him on our calendar, time with Him is often the first thing that we drop.

Family is important. You're reading this, so I have to assume you agree. Yet, just as we unpacked with our God time, while we often say we value our family, do we schedule *around* or *regardless of* our family time? If we are married, are we ensuring we have time alone as a couple? Scheduling date nights, weekends away, and extended vacations together ensures that our calendar reflects our priority of having a strong marriage. Likewise, for those of us with kids, are we guaranteeing quality time together with the priority of building up a strong family?

Quality time is different than quantity time, isn't it? Not all time spent is time spent well. Being in the same room as someone, especially our kids, does not automatically equal quality time. More often than I'd like to admit, I find myself aimlessly wandering down a rabbit trail on my phone while my kids are left longing for time and attention. It is one thing to make sure we have time together and quite another thing to make that time valuable.

Tiffani and I know it can be easy for us to get caught up in housework or whatever project might be hanging over our heads at home. To make up for our shortcomings, we find value in being on "vacation." This can take any number of forms. For instance, we will do day trips together, weekends away camping, and take as many road trips as possible together. But we are also working on developing more intentional stay-cations where we can put our attention on doing things together as a family instead of drifting back into house and office work, not to mention any number of other distractions.

On the chalkboard wall in our kitchen, my girls keep a running record of who is next up for a daddy-daughter date. These typically involve going out for breakfast before church or having lunch together. We also have a rotation of going to sporting events or concerts. But it's not just me. Tiffani has her own list of daughter dates she keeps track of on the chalkboard wall.

Why do we do this? Well, we believe in spending time together as a couple, as a family, and dating our daughters as individuals. All of these things are a priority for us. Because they're a priority, we put them in our calendars to ensure they happen. It's not a perfect rhythm, but we are learning to be intentional about spending time together. We want our calendars to reflect the priority we place on family.

Serving together as a family teaches our kids the value Jesus placed on loving and serving others. We can often teach our kids best by bringing them along with us and letting them watch what, how, and why we do things.

BRIAN SCHLEY

Tiffani had been volunteering at our local domestic violence shelter when she decided to model this idea of bringing and watching. She didn't want this to be something she would do alone, so she found an opportunity to take our kids with her. She established an opportunity to give parents who were living at the shelter a break by taking their kids outside, playing games, and setting up activities for them. Our daughters joined in the planning and activities with the other kids. They witnessed firsthand what it was like for their Mom to serve kids in the shelter. Tiffani was able to share with them, at an age-appropriate level, why families were in the shelter. They watched how she loved on the kids there. They watched how she played with them. They absorbed her love for serving others. It is one thing to tell our kids it is important to serve. It is another thing to show them.

Our calendars reflect our values. Our kids will understand our values by what we spend our time on, not based on what we tell them our values are. And at this very moment, they are establishing their values based on our calendars. What do our calendars reveal about our values? What do our kids see in us?

Cash

Cash, credit cards, checkbooks—I am talking about any form of currency. The form is less important than the value it represents. How do you spend your money? As with time, if you want to get a better view of your values, look at your bank account. Where do your funds go? Do they reflect the values you want to honor? What do your kids see you spend your finances on? What do you want them to grow up spending their finances on?

Money is a different type of resource than time. With time, we are on equal footing. We all have the same amount of time to spend each day. But when it comes to money, our resources vary from one home to the next. Regardless, as families chasing after Jesus, we have the same obligation to spend it God's way.

Finances are a frequent flyer when it comes to topics covered in the Bible. God knows how we are wired and knew we would need many reminders and instructions about how to deal with our finances. Either money will control us, or we will control it. If we control it, we view it as a tool to use and not an idol to long for. That's worth a pause, don't you think? In this season of life, is money a tool in your home and heart or an idol?

How we currently spend our finances will give us insight into what we value. Certainly, we all spend some portion of our income on necessary things like housing, transportation, and food. And most of us spend another good-sized portion on entertainment in and outside of the home. Yet, when we look at our budget breakdown, our values tend to be revealed. We can compare two families with similar incomes and watch them spend their money very differently. Some value their home and will put a larger percentage of income there. Others value their vehicles and will put more there. For some, money is to be invested, and a chunk of change will go toward future savings or spending. We all currently spend according to our values, even if we have not put much thought into it.

Tiffani and I have enjoyed traveling together since before we had kids. It is a value we share that has not shifted throughout our marriage. We believe in spending time together and doing so somewhere other than home. We love road trips, seeing the countryside, and doing so with our loved ones. Not to mention, we're fortunate to have family and friends in places we love to visit. Family and friends who are crazy enough to put our family of seven up for a few nights at a time.

Some people will look at us and question how we could possibly vacation so much. They may consider such spending frivolous, but for us, it represents a value we hold dearly. In order to spend more on trips, we have had to make sacrifices in other areas. For example, our vehicles each currently have around a quarter million miles on them. The value we place on vehicles is quite minimal. I want them to get me from point A to point B, but they will be well-used and well-loved. We also try to keep our monthly costs down. That means we don't have cable TV or any sort of subscription service, just a few local channels that come through the antenna. We all spend differently. Not right or wrong, but different. As parents, we must assess how our spending habits reflect our values.

Now, there's the current way we spend money, and then there's the way we want to move forward. Tiffani and I agree we want to spend according to God's values. We want to make sure we give our first fruits back to God, entrusting him to lead us on how, when, and where to spend the rest. We strive to be generous to God and others, as He has certainly been generous to us. For me, that often means deferring to my wife when it comes to generosity. She is naturally more generous than I am, so when we are approached with an opportunity to financially give, I will often defer to whatever "number" she feels led to share.

We also strive to teach generosity to our kids. We include them in our discussions on generosity. Each of our girls has piggy banks divided into three different sections: save, spend, and share. They place a percentage of what they receive from birthdays, chores, or other side jobs into the share bank. Then, when our family is approached with what we deem to be a good opportunity to support, we include them in it. For instance, we have had the opportunity to support two former youth ministry students who were each going away on mission for a year. Before deciding what to give, I invited each to our home where they could present what they would be doing to our family. Afterward, each of my kids had the opportunity to consider how much they would give from their share banks. We also let them know how much their Mom and I would be giving to help teach them how we decide to be generous. If we expect them to be generous, we also have to be generous. In order for them to know about our generosity, they need to be included in it and taught how we discern and decide.

We have also had family discussions surrounding what we give to when opportunities emerge. We let our kiddos know that we receive many requests from all sorts of individuals and organizations for money, and we want them to know which ones we say yes to and why. After all, we have boundaries around the things we're willing to support, and we want our girls to understand them. While not overly restrictive, we look for two distinctives: God and relationships. We want to support things that are a movement of God. We want to support the Gospel going forth. We also want to support people we are in relationship with, which means we want to support our family and friends in what they're doing. Not every request receives a yes from us, but we want to be generous where and when possible.

How we spend our cash reveals our values. From saving to monthly expenses to generosity, values-based finances are something our kids will learn from us. Our kids are growing up understanding what is important based on how we spend money. What do your kids currently see in your spending? What do we want them to see?

Conversations

Our words matter. They, too, are a resource. And what we say impacts both those we are talking with and those who are close enough to hear. Our kids will fall into both of those categories. What we say to them, they take notice of. What we say around them, even when we don't think they're listening, they also take notice of.

You can imagine what we say reveals what we value, just as it does with our time and money. Jesus said, "For the mouth speaks out of that which fills the heart" (Luke 6:45). Stated another way, "For whatever is in your heart determines what you say" (Luke 6:45 NLT). The words we say and the conversations we have spill out of what fills our hearts. Our values are reflected in the conversations we have with people, and our kids will grab ahold of our values based on what we say. What are you saying? What values are they hearing?

If we take after Jairus and run after Jesus only to fall at His feet, how will that earnest desire and action come out in our speech? In other words, if we approach our faith with a Jairus-like desire to dive into reading Scripture, it will be like putting God's Word directly into our hearts. Which means that when our kids hear us speak, they'll hear the Scripture on our hearts pouring out of our mouths.

Tiffani and I have been part of small groups at church since before we had kids. Our family has grown from a family of two to a family of seven, all the while doing life with others in small groups. Most years, we have met in homes with other families while kids are in laps, watching movies, or playing in the next room. Some years, we met as babysitters watched the kids, giving the adults freedom to talk without interruption. Through it all, our kids have understood that we are meeting with other adults to talk about the Bible, to talk about life, and to pray with one another. They've listened in on our conversations and joined in on times of prayer. Our kids and those from other families have watched us sit in living rooms, at kitchen tables, in backyards, at parades, and while serving together, talk about life and faith.

Clearly I don't always get it right, like instructing my daughter to punch her sister. Despite my shortcomings, words matter. Despite our shortcomings as parents, we can aspire to chase God with all our heart, mind, soul, and strength. And as we do, we can watch when that passion overflows from our mouths into our conversations.

Every day, I have to be intentional, asking myself, when faced with the opportunity, am I willing to bring God into my conversations today? It's worth some time of reflection, don't you think? Does our faith spew out of our mouths when we talk, or is it muted or missing? When others ask how we are doing, instead of answering with the automatic "Good," what if we responded with, "Man, God has been good to me. Can I tell you about it?" Or, when someone tells you they are struggling, can you ask to pray for them? When someone clues you in on a difficult decision they have to make, how would it feel to suggest that God may have something to say about their future and what He has planned for them?

The more we have conversations that focus on God, the more our kids will hear us and absorb what we talk about. As they grow up in a home where this is the norm, well, we may have the opportunity to hear similar conversations come out of their mouths as they grow.

CONCLUSION

Have you ever used the line, "Do as I say, not as I do?" In parenting, that doesn't work. But you probably already know that from experience by now. Our kids want to follow us—what we say and do. Telling them to do things differently than how we're truly living is confusing.

Jairus went after Jesus. When he was desperate, he ran to Jesus and didn't stop until he found Him. Like I said in the last chapter, I don't believe it was the first time he ran to Jesus. It wasn't a shot in the dark at healing his daughter. Jairus went after the person he knew could bring life to his daughter. Like our kids will with us, Jairus knew Jesus could help because he had been learning from Jesus and overhearing what He had been doing around the countryside. Jairus believed in what Jesus had to say and lived a life that reflected it.

He personally brought Jesus to his daughter, and she was saved because of it. What Jairus did for his child, we can do for ours. We can follow Jairus' way of running after Jesus and letting our lives spill over into our kids.

This might sound ominous, but it's worth saying, considering that it bears itself out time and again. As parents, we will not be effective if we tell our kids that Jesus is important without actually following Him. We will not be effective when we tell our kids that church is important but aren't making the effort to show the value of attending regularly and engaging deeply. We will not effectively teach our kids about serving without our example of serving others. And we will not be effective in teaching our kids about grace and forgiveness if they don't see us modeling it within our walls, offering it to them, or displaying it with others.

If we want our kids to follow in our footsteps, we have to ask ourselves if we are walking the paths we want them to walk. Are they seeing in us what we want them to become? We want to be able to look at them and say, "Do as I say and do what I do."

BRIAN SCHLEY

1. Jairus ran to Jesus and fell at His feet. What has it looked like in your life, running after Jesus and falling at His feet? Do your kids see you chasing Jesus and falling at His feet?

2. Our kids follow in our footsteps. In what ways are you glad that your kids follow you? In what areas are you hopeful they won't?

3. Our kids see and mimic what we value. What are your top three to five values? How are you consciously living them out?

4. If you were to take an objective look at your calendar, cash, and conversations, how would these areas reflect your values?

5. What specific and attainable step will you take to bring your calendar, cash, and conversations more in line with the person God is calling you to be?

3 They Are Not Our Kids

What do we do in the waiting? Waiting is hard. Waiting to get results to find out whether or not Sophie's cancer had returned was extremely hard. All we wanted to know was what was next, yet everything seemed to be going in slow motion. The waiting brought with it impatience, frustration, anger, bitterness, and many other adjectives that would not be found as fruits of the Spirit. While it revealed our shortcomings, it also revealed a deep longing to simply trust God with what He has entrusted us with.

God has given us our kids—temporarily. We have been entrusted with His children to teach them about Him throughout all of our days in all we do. As a dad, I have a role to play. Yet, if I'm being honest, oftentimes, I try to not only play my role but His as well. And if you're anything like me, you want to control, dictate, and demand what you want in *your* way and in *your* timing.

Like I said, waiting is hard. While we wait on health results, our kids to grow in maturity, or for them to put their faith in Jesus, our impatience is revealed along with our lack of trust. As our kids continue to grow up, we have to continue to trust Jesus with them. They're not ours. They're His. They are on loan for a while. God has entrusted us to do our part. The question is, will we trust Him to do His part?

JAIRUS WAITS

Jairus did what he set out to do. He accomplished the unimaginable upon leaving his house that morning. Not only did he find Jesus, but he convinced Him to come to help his daughter. He pleaded his case to Jesus. He told Jesus that she was on the verge of death. But he also shared his overwhelming faith, declaring that if Jesus would just come and lay a hand on her, well, Jairus believed she would fully spring to life. After hearing Jairus speak, Jesus simply got up and followed Jairus to his house.

At that point, Jairus must have felt victorious. He must have been nervously joyful as Jesus turned to follow him. Hopeful anticipation growing.

That joyful feeling was no doubt quickly met with anxiety. Just as Jesus began to follow Jairus, He stopped, saying, "Who touched my garments?" (Mark 5:30). The crowd stood still. People were all over. The streets were packed. Jesus brought with Him a traffic jam of people everywhere He went. People were constantly bumping into one another and touching his clothing. Yet, this time, He stopped the crowd to ask who had touched his clothes.

If you're Jairus, what are you thinking at this point? "You've got to be nuts, Jesus. Who touched you? It could be fifty different people. What does it matter? Let's go! We have to get to my daughter!"

In the middle of this great story of Jairus and his family, the Bible introduces us to a young woman who has had a health issue of bleeding for twelve straight years. She is quite familiar with waiting. We're told that she had gone to many doctors and undoubtedly prayed many prayers for healing. Now, she finally had the opportunity to approach Jesus in desperation. Sound familiar? She had run out of options, and the current one was simple—touch a piece of Jesus' clothing. She simply thought if she could just touch a piece of Jesus' clothing, she could be healed.

She did not say anything to Jesus. She did not get in front of Him and stop the procession heading to Jairus' home. She simply snuck up from behind, drew in close, and touched the corner of his robe.

Jesus knew what had happened. He felt it. And despite being committed to Jairus' struggle, He stopped everybody in their tracks and asked, "Who touched my garment?"

She was stunned. Everyone was stunned. She had been caught.

Gripped with fear, she trembled, then spoke. She told Jesus about her twelve years of suffering. She told Him about all of the doctors and all the attempts to heal her and how it left her broke and worse off. She admitted her plan, that if she could simply touch Him, she believed she would be healed.

And she was right.

Her faith healed her.

Jesus acknowledged her and her faith and her long wait. After twelve years of suffering, she believed it was Jesus who could finally heal her.

BRIAN SCHLEY

I wonder if Jairus heard any of the conversation between Jesus and this woman. It's possible he missed the whole ordeal, mumbling under his breath about needing to get moving. That time was wasting away. After all, his daughter was his concern. "Nice story, lady. Now Jesus, can we get out of here?!"

There is something about waiting that is beautiful. There is something about waiting that causes us to understand we are not in control. When we are forced to wait on God's perfect timing, we are thrown into an often uncomfortable and yet beautiful space in life. We have the opportunity to look up to God, open our hands in full submission, and let Him take over.

Jesus had already told Jairus He was going to his house. Jairus plead his case. Jesus heard it and gave his response. Jesus even acted on his response. Reflecting on this, I had to wonder if that was enough to calm Jairus' heart and trust Jesus to do what only Jesus can do? Are we, parents, okay with doing our job and trusting Jesus to do His?

GIVE TIME & SPACE—IN TIME

It didn't take long for panic to set in. The teenage girls next to us on the beach asked if our daughter was the one wearing the pink swimsuit. As we told them she was and quickly glanced at where Sophie had been building a sandcastle, we noticed she wasn't there. They let us know they had watched her walk down the beach. Panic.

Our group quickly stood up and yelled for her. Tiffani and her cousin ran in the direction the girls had pointed. I went in the opposite direction to talk with the lifeguard.

The lifeguard was cool, calm, and collected. He was a young man, but it was clear this wasn't the first time he had this type of conversation. He assured me it would be just fine and that this happens multiple times each day. He mentioned that it's usually quicker when a kid approaches a lifeguard to find lost parents because parents are typically frantic. But when parents, such as us, are looking for kids, it can take a few minutes before kids even realize that they're lost.

Shortly after, I watched as my wife returned with our youngest. Like the lifeguard predicted, Sophie was clueless she was lost in the first place. In her frequent trips filling her bucket with water from the ocean to her sandcastle, she got a little turned around and went to where she thought we were sitting. And then just continued to walk in that direction. She was a solid football field down the beach.

We were no more than twenty feet away from her when we took our eyes off her. We watched her, over and over, go from the water to her sandcastle for an hour. We assumed she had her path memorized. In that moment, we handed over the responsibility of her well-being from us to her. Sophie wasn't ready for it. Granted, she was young, just four and a half years old. We trusted her to have a general sense of direction and understanding of where we were in relation to the ocean. At her age, it was too much trust, too soon. Now, if she were fourteen and a half and we were still monitoring her every move from the sandcastle to the ocean, that may be a little excessive. There has to be a happy medium somewhere in there, right?

Joseph and Mary may have found their happy medium when Jesus was twelve years old. When we feel bad about letting our kiddo wander down the beach for a couple minutes, all we have to do is read Luke 2:41-52 and be reassured. Why? Because

Joseph and Mary, the earthly parents of the Messiah, lost Jesus for three days!

Joseph and Mary had given Jesus the freedom and responsibility of going to The Temple to learn from the teachers. They had departed Jerusalem that day with a large caravan. Joseph would have traveled with the men, and Mary would have traveled with the women at different times throughout each day. Each one had assumed Jesus was with the other. Classic miscommunication. By the time they realized Jesus was missing, they had been traveling all day and hunkered down for the evening. Makes me wonder if that was an awkward time of prayer for Joseph and Mary. "God, yeah, well, we kind of lost your Son, you know, the Savior of the world. We could use a little help here."

When Joseph and Mary found Jesus in the temple several days later, He was patiently sitting there, learning from the teachers. As they expressed how they had been worried sick and frantically searching for Him, He simply asked, "Why is it that you were looking for Me? Did you not know that I had to be in My Father's house?" (Luke 2:49). Jesus, a budding teenager, had hit a level of maturity. He understood His role. He understood who His Father was. His parents were forced to learn that He could be trusted in His faith journey. That He was capable of understanding and acting on what was most important.

Maybe, at twelve, our youngest will be entrusted with big, faith-filled decisions in similar fashion. I also hope Tiffani and I do a better job at communicating with one another when it comes to recognizing the maturity shift when it's happening. And, of course, we'd rather not leave her behind for several days unnoticed on any given trip. That said, as parents, we fully understand there will come a day when we will be able to trust our kids to take their faith into their own hands. Even if they end up wandering off course a bit.

CENTERING JESUS

HELICOPTER LANDING

When a child is missing, even for a moment, it is terrifying. When something bad happens to them, our natural reaction is to encase them in a giant bubble and never let them out of our sight again. Over the years, "helicopter parents" have received a bad rap. Helicopter parents are known for hovering above their kids, never letting them out of sight, and never giving them too much room to explore this world on their own.

I understand why parents fly around above their kids. It gives us assurance that they're okay. After all, one of our biggest jobs as parents is to make sure our kids are alive and well.

But let me throw some caution to our helicopter wind. Yes, we ought to look out for their safety, but just as important, we need to evaluate our hovering and ask, "Is this what's best for our kids, or is this what's best for me?" We can choose to hover in a given situation or season, believing it is what's best for our kids. That's great. However, that's not always the case, is it? We can also parent in ways that simply benefit us. It makes us feel better when we hover. It calms our anxious thoughts and fears. We feel needed and valued when we are out there protecting our kids.

Do you remember the day you became a parent? When we become parents, our lives are forever changed. I remember leaving the hospital with Brinley. After spending a couple days in the hospital and learning from the nurses everything I would need to know in the short term, we were ready to be discharged. I went to our car to securely fasten the new and mysterious car seat. It was a cool March day in Wisconsin, sunny and probably in the forties, but there I was, dripping sweat like an out-of-shape contortionist pulling on that car seat as tight as I could possibly muscle it. That thing wasn't going to budge. I was told it should be tight, so I was going to make sure it was, in fact, tight. Then came the time to put our first baby in that car seat and drive away. My head was on a swivel, spinning faster than I ever remember, just trying to get out of the parking lot. It didn't take long before my forearms began cramping up as I white-knuckled that steering wheel, sensitive to every movement around me. The first couple minutes on the road told me a lot about my new role and the weight of responsibility I felt.

How do we handle this weight of responsibility?

It feels good to be wanted and needed by our kids. But at what point do we need to stop cutting the edges off the PBJs we packed them for lunch? When is it time for them to order food at the restaurant or sell their school fundraiser items? The decisions we make as parents, big and small, either facilitate their growth into adulthood or simply, and selfishly, I might add, allow us to continue to feel needed.

If we are not careful, we might end up white-knuckling the helicopter around our kids for the rest of their lives. Can you hear the warning alarms buzzing at the thought of that? If we choose to fly that way, we may not allow them to grow into the individuals God is shaping them to be. We are given caterpillars with the goal of sending butterflies from our homes. If we never let them flap their wings, they'll be living with us forever. As much fun as that might sound to some of us, that is not the goal.

GRACE PLAYS THE LONG GAME

God has patiently entrusted us with our kids. His kids. We, in turn, need to trust Him with them. While Jairus was able to meet Jesus face-to-face and recruit Him to come into his home and help his daughter, the timing was not up to Jairus. Jesus had control over that entire situation, knew what the outcome would be, and decided it was okay to pause in order to minister to the young woman. Although it may have only been a matter of minutes, I can only assume it felt like hours to Jairus. God tends to be more patient than we are.

God is full of grace and patience. We tend to lack in both areas. God plays the long game. I'm often focused on the immediate. His grace is sufficient for us. His grace is sufficient for our kids. And His grace was sufficient for Jairus' daughter two thousand years ago. In that moment, Jairus was forced to be more patient than he would have wanted. He had to trust Jesus in the process. After all, there was nothing more Jairus could do but wait patiently.

As parents, we're smothered with opportunities to feel like Jairus, where there is nothing more we can do but place our faith and trust in Jesus while waiting to watch Him work in our kids' lives.

The testing of our patience as we attempt to trust God to take care of our kids isn't an if but a when. It's part of the parent-child contract.

When Brinley was a baby, she didn't like to sleep much. We entered into parenthood oblivious to the fact that some babies actually sleep at night. Fortunately, she simply paved the way for the next two, as neither slept through the night until they were at least fourteen months old. Tiffani and I worked to balance doing night shifts while maintaining some form of sanity. We started by alternating who got up throughout the night. This didn't last long. The problem was that we would end up elbowing one another, saying, "I was just up. It's your turn." The reality was we were both "just up" because we were up multiple times throughout the night. What was the solution? We settled on a first-shift / second-shift option. Before two a.m. and after two a.m. That way, we could at least look at the clock and know who was supposed to be up.

If people were quiet about these things, we would never have known that some kids actually sleep through the night. However, some people like to openly brag about their sleeping beauties, and it didn't take long for us to realize that not every parent was fighting the same level of sleep deprivation we were. As people shared with us how their kids slept through the night, I found myself wanting to slap them and learn from them at the same time. I don't recall ever slapping anyone, but then again, I was sleep-deprived.

As a first-time parent, I remember telling my boss about our sleep issues. We had been reading all sorts of articles, getting book recommendations, and trying to learn from anyone what we were doing wrong. Having adult children, she calmly looked at me and said, "Brian, my kids sleep just fine right now. Time will go quick. She will start to sleep at some point. You're not doing anything wrong. Just try to enjoy the time you get rocking her at night."

Grace plays the long game. Sleeping through the night seemed like a forever game when we were in it. But, as you can imagine, she eventually started to sleep through the night. Looking back, I do miss those nights rocking my baby girl through the quiet hours of the night.

We want our kids to sleep through the night, but it takes time. Grace plays the long game.

We want our kids to understand how to manage their emotions and not react in anger with their siblings. Grace plays the long game.

We want their faith to be their own and not simply follow in our footsteps. Grace plays the long game.

We want our kids to be open about sharing their faith with friends, classmates, or teammates. Guess what? Grace plays the long game.

CONSISTENCY WINS THE LONG GAME

While we wait, consistency will pay off. The tendency, while we long for our kids to draw near to God or mature in their faith journey in some capacity, will be to look to try new things or alter our methods. At times, change may be needed, but we serve a God who is the same from beginning to end. He is the model of consistency. Consistent parenting over a long period will reveal to our kids the same thing we see in God as He is consistent—we are trustworthy, dependable, reliable, and true to our word. Our kids will continue to see us as beacons of light in our faith journey, in our beliefs, and in our methods as they are consistently rooted in the Bible. Consistency will allow our kids the freedom to feel comfortable knowing they can test the waters and explore as they seek to understand this world and their faith. Our consistency provides them the opportunity to be confident in having a home base that doesn't move. As the prodigal son found out in Luke 15:11-32, he had a home to return to that was consistent. Not shunned, cut off, or scolded when he left, he felt welcome to return home. His father's love never changed. Even as our kids wander or stray, we can remain consistent. Consistency wins.

Consistency in prayer is essential in our lives, particularly during the waiting game. As parents, we will need to draw near to Jesus daily as we continue to learn to trust Him. And if we're serious about prayerfully taking on the battles in our kids' lives, then turning to Him is our only hope.

We can try all we want and as hard as we want to help our kids, but a minute of prayer can do more than a day filled with stress and lectures. When we have a longing for our kids, we turn to Jesus. When our kids are struggling, we turn to Jesus. When we are living in uncertainty, we turn to Jesus.

Going to Jesus in prayer helps two people. First, we are helping ourselves. After all, we are in need of support, encouragement, and comfort when our kids are going through challenges. Our parent heartstrings get pulled hard. We wish we could take away hurt, pain, or trial, all the while longing for our kids to make good choices, be healthy, and enjoy right relationships with peers and with God. When they struggle, whether our kids realize it or not, our strings are getting pulled. Of course, it would be nice if we could just push a "fix it" button where everything turned perfect and joyful. While that would be fantastic, we have something better—an open invitation to be with Jesus during these times. What's more, we need to turn to Him since we share the burden of our kids' struggles.

Second, when we go to Jesus in prayer, we are helping our kids. We know He can do more than we ever could, yet we can default to relying on our strength and determination instead of His power and discernment. Remember, God loves our kids more than we do. He wants their very best. As they go through life, He wants them to grow closer to Him, to rely on Him, to listen to Him, and to grow in knowledge of Him. God will use the little and big things in life to draw our kids closer to Him. And we want them to rely on Him, don't we?

Along with trusting our kids with more of life's responsibilities, we are also trusting God to watch over them. Striking that balance will be important. We don't want to smother them to the point where they can't function well on their own. But we also want to be cautious about giving them too much responsibility too soon.

I don't know about you, but I can put a lot of pressure on myself to raise our kids to love God and become responsible adults.

Tiffani shared with me the burden she feels to raise our daughters to be the women God has called them to be. We see the years ticking by as they race toward that magic number, eighteen. Now, we certainly won't be kicking them out at eighteen, but at that point, they will be deciding, hopefully with our support, what their future looks like. Right now, we can see that they're not there yet. We can see the areas we need to continue to help them grow to be functioning adults in this world. The pressure is real. Yet, as Tiffani shared her burden, I couldn't help but think of God's role in raising our kids. So, I did what any good husband would do and spoke without fully considering what I was about to say. Looking at my wife, I said, "Honey, you're just not that important." Boldly yet humbly, I continued to elaborate. I told her she was discrediting the work God would do in our kids and through us. I reminded her and myself that He loves them more than we do.

We have the tendency to get caught up in the here and now. We struggle to see the forest through the trees. God doesn't. He sees the big picture. He knows the beginning from the end. You and me? We tend to focus on right now. When we do, we can lose focus on the long game—the eternal game. Grace plays the long game. God plays the long game. We need to remind ourselves that we serve a God who loves our kids dearly. He wants their very best, as do we. Yet, we tend to leave Him out of our parenting.

Turn to Him. Talk to Him. Ask Him for help—for you and your kids.

BRIAN SCHLEY

PREPARE THEM FOR THE LONG GAME

In order to fully talk out of both sides of my mouth, let me propose we are extremely important in helping our kids grow up and develop into the people God has intended them to be. I know. I just suggested to my wife that she's just not that important. That, also, is true. We need to understand God's role along with ours in this whole parenting thing. His is vital. Ours is valuable.

I'm raising my girls with the long game in mind. I am not raising infants, toddlers, tweens, or teens. Tiffani and I are raising adults-in-the-making. What do they need in order to be productive, contributing, Jesus-loving adults at each phase of their lives on the road to adulthood?

When they're young, we help them pour milk into their sippy cups. As they grow, they understand the tipping point of a gallon of milk and figure out how to do it on their own. When they're young, we let them use butter knives with dull edges because they just aren't capable of using them correctly without risking a trip to the ER. Yet, at some point, we begin to teach them and monitor their ability to use a sharp knife. If they're going to survive beyond our home, they have to learn how to move beyond sippy cups and butter knives. But they have to do so in appropriate seasons.

We are country dwellers. We live on a couple acres with land that connects to our property where we can take hikes, explore the woods, and ride ATVs. Our girls have been riding on ATVs since they were tiny humans. They started riding with me and their mom from the time they could hold their heads up—one arm wrapped around them as they sat in front of us between our legs. As they grew, they progressed to riding behind us, holding onto our waist. When they were ready, we'd switch again to riding behind them. Only now, they would take the handles and drive with our support. As they showed us they had the ability to control the ATV, handling it in a safe manner, only then would they go off on their own.

It dawned on me one day, as I watched my then ten-year-old flying around the yard on an ATV that she certainly had the ability to drive our riding lawn mower. Calling Brinley over, I shared my new epiphany with her and immediately showed her how to use the lawn mower. From that moment on, she started to cut the lawn. Brinley was more than happy to be doing something she deemed only "mature" people could do. I was thrilled I no longer had to cut the lawn. She was growing up. It was a slow progression from ATV to lawn mower, but just like teaching her to sleep through the night, it slowly happened quickly.

We are playing the long game where we gradually release responsibility as they continue to grow in understanding, maturity, and wisdom. It is important to strike a balance between holding them back and giving them too much too soon. It would have been irresponsible on my part to put Brinley on the lawn mower at age ten if she had not been comfortable riding a machine before. It would be irresponsible to not let her cut the lawn if she was fully capable.

What we did with Brinley in regards to lawn cutting and pouring milk is referred to as the I Do – We Do – You Do method. I do a task, and my kids watch and learn. We do it together for accountability and fine-tuning. Finally, they do it on their own. I drove the ATV, and she would sit with me and watch me drive it. We did it together where she took the handles, with my arms over the top, and she started to learn to steer with my help. Eventually, she was set free to ride on her own. We can utilize the I Do – We

Do – You Do method in many areas of parenting as we slowly teach them how to manage life's tasks. No doubt you are already thinking through areas where you could have leaned on this model. Don't worry. There's more to come.

How does that scenario play out in other, more challenging ways? Technology is a huge component our kids are navigating from early on. It is a blessing and a curse. There are so many positive uses we have with technology. I love being able to see my kids from one screen to another, even when we may be many miles apart. Yet, this same technology gets kids in a bind when not used appropriately. If we pay any attention to news reports or emerging studies, we understand that social media, pictures, videos and other avenues can be used to exploit kids in the worst possible ways. Our teens can be asked or coerced into sharing pictures or videos of themselves in provocative ways. How do we follow the same principles as we play the long game to help our kids navigate technology, dating, friendships, or any other area that can be hazardous as they progress to maturity?

Play the long game and understand the appropriate release of responsibility. We don't hand kids phones at a young age and let them explore. We give boundaries. We let them watch what we do. They explore as we look over their shoulders. They start taking off on their own while we watch and monitor. We tell them where they can and can't go. We pray that as they continue to navigate any of these tricky areas, God watches over them and us and that they learn to understand for themselves what is good and what is harmful.

The easy thing would be to let our kids do whatever they want.

The easy thing is to give in.

Because arguing, boundary setting, and constantly saying "No" is difficult. We can get worn down. We can want a break to navigate our personal lives—work, chores, projects, friendships, etc.—so handing our kids a screen or letting them do whatever they want can sound like a nice break for us, and you know what? It could be. But, oftentimes, the easy thing is not the best thing.

This is difficult stuff. Speaking from experience, the challenges presented to parents in navigating these issues are a struggle. When we hear, "But everyone else's parents let them do this," how do we respond? Do we accept the idea that we don't want to be the only parents with unreasonable boundaries, or do we double down on the belief that we are doing the right thing? Personally, I'm open to considering where we may be too strict, too loose, or just haven't considered all the facets thoroughly enough. I'm also perfectly fine being the "only parent" who doesn't allow something. The thing is, I'm not responsible for other parents' kids. I'm responsible for the kids God has entrusted to me. And ultimately, I'm responsible to Him for how I parent. Sometimes, the hard thing to do is to hold the line. Sometimes, we need to do the hard thing. Our kids need to do hard things too. Truth is, it's all part of the long game. We just have to trust God to teach us and them how to work through the hard parts of this life.

CONCLUSION

God doesn't have spiritual grandchildren.

The first time I heard this line, I remember having to pause and think it through. God only has spiritual children. If we are a child of God, our children are not God's grandchildren. He doesn't operate that way. He only has kids, not grandkids. Our faith doesn't get passed down to our kids just because we have faith. At some point—we pray—our kids put their faith in Jesus as we have. We can do all we can to put them in an environment to hear and see Jesus at work, but it is still their decision whether or not to trust in Him.

I want my kids to love Jesus.

I want them to love God's Word.

I want to make them read their Bibles

I'd love it if they turned to Him in prayer before they turned to me.

My hope is that they surround themselves with great friends who help point them toward Jesus in good times and bad. If they desire to follow His will above theirs or mine, I will be ecstatic. I want to lead a life that points them toward Him. I want them to see me reading His Word, talking with Him, and loving people the way He loves us. I want them to see their Heavenly Father the way I do.

God has entrusted us with His children, not His grandchildren. So, we do our part while they're in our homes and let God do His part as we work together to teach our children about the love He has for them. We are patient. We don't hover. We lead. We are consistent. We trust. We love.

3   REFLECTION QUESTIONS

1. Have you ever had a season of "waiting" on the Lord? As you reflect on that period, what did waiting do for your faith journey?

2. How do you strike a balance between hovering over and allowing for independence? Do you have a method for discerning when it is time to give your kids more control?

3. Consistency over a long period impacts our kids. What things have you been consistent with in your parenting? Are there areas in which you would like to start being more consistent personally or within your marriage?

4. The value of praying for our kids cannot be overstated. In what ways would you like to be praying for your child—in the present and for the future? Have you considered keeping a journal of your prayers?

5. How would you explain God's role and your role in parenting? What is God responsible for? What are you responsible for?

CENTERING JESUS

4   Everyone is Doing It

Tiffani and I often consider ourselves overprotective parents. Well, that's partially true. Our kids, and maybe a few of their friends, believe we are overprotective parents. We just consider ourselves, well, parents.

I don't consider myself an overprotective parent in all settings. Tiffani would not consider me an overprotective parent in all scenarios either. When she came home after work one evening and found our kids pulling one another in sleds behind our ATV with a few jump ropes tied together that they found in the garage and with a proud dad watching, she wouldn't have considered me overprotective, much less a parent in that moment. I, however, believed they were brilliantly problem-solving new ways to have fun! Protective parenting is relative.

Typically, we want to know the kids and parents of the friends our girls hang out with. Our desire is that their family values, within reason, match ours. With young kids, especially during the elementary years, it is not uncommon for kids to invite many of their classmates over for birthday parties. On the one hand, it's great to see kids connect so easily. On the other, it can be difficult to discern the values of other families through brief interactions at parties.

Early on, one of our girls had been invited to a birthday party at a classmate's house. It sounded like all the girls in the class were invited. We did not know the family, and my wife scarcely recognized the girl from volunteering in their classroom. This was one of those tricky calls. Our daughter desperately wanted to go to the party where "everyone in her class was going"—yeah, that line gets used at a younger age than I would like.

We figured we would play it by ear. My wife dropped her off at the birthday girl's house, got out and introduced herself to the parents, then stayed around a bit in order to scope things out. She then left to run a few errands. My phone rang. She relayed a few things to me about the birthday party. Kids from class were there, and so were extended family members. The adults seemed to be having a great time indulging in food, beverages, and music. Given the types of conversations that were being had, music being listened to, and alcohol being consumed, my wife didn't have a warm, fuzzy feeling about leaving our girl there too long. So, her trip to run errands became a quick jaunt out and an early pickup at the party. She returned and let the parents know she was there to pick up our daughter and wished the little girl a happy birthday and a fun time for all who remained.

We didn't know what to expect when dropping our little girl off at a stranger's house. The whole notion of letting her go in the first place was a bit of a stretch for us, but we decided, at least this time, to give it a shot. So, we developed a quick exit strategy.

As the years have gone on, the exit strategies have flipped. This time for one of our middle schoolers. She knew the girl from school, but not very well. And though she didn't know the family, she felt comfortable going to their house. Not knowing how long she would want to stay, her plan, after cluing us in on her reasoning, was to cut her time at the party short. She wanted to go for two hours rather than stay the entire time. If she was feeling really comfortable and having a blast, she would call and ask to stay later. If not, I would get her as planned.

This was now her plan. I really liked her plan. Having talked through these situations early in life has led her to consider them as she grows up. I still dropped her off and introduced myself to the family. This time, however, I felt really comfortable with them. Of course, I also stalked them on social media beforehand. You know, the usual dad stuff. When she was young, Tiffani and I were fully in charge of the planning. Now? She's figuring out what works for her based on her comfort level tied to our values. After I picked her up, she said she had a great time and would like to hang out with her again.

We are the gatekeepers. When our kids were young, we kept the gate narrow. As they've gotten older, they understand what the gate looks like as far as who should be let in. Now, as they mature, it doesn't mean we abandon our post as gatekeepers with who we let into our kids' lives. On the contrary, it means our goal is to transfer wisdom over to them so we can stand by and watch them open and close the gate. It's that You Do part of our training method. Yet, while they're still young, we hold fast to the keys.

JESUS THE GATEKEEPER (Mark 5:39-40; Matthew 9:23-25)

Jesus was a gatekeeper at Jairus' home. When they arrived,

Jesus asked why everyone was crying since, according to Him, the girl had simply fallen asleep. With that, the people began to laugh. Taking note of their reaction, Jesus actively became the gatekeeper and kicked everyone out. All those who were not filled with hope for the girl and unwilling to believe that Jesus could save her were no longer welcome in Jairus' home. Jesus controlled the gate, and in this scenario, He kept people out.

After Jesus removed people from the home, He selected those who would enter the gate with Him, choosing Jairus and his wife, along with Peter, James, and John. The people Jesus allowed into Jairus' home to be part of saving his daughter's life included those who believed in who Jesus was and what He could do. At least, I'm assuming that Dad and Mom believed Jesus could save their daughter. Why else would they have searched Him out and implored Him to come to their home? The moment they invited Jesus in, they released control of the gate. Having control of the gate, He only allowed certain people in.

Jesus gave us the model to follow, didn't he? If we want to bring Him into our homes, we need to be gatekeepers in line with His values. We need to limit those who come in and only welcome those who will positively impact our kids' lives.

Kids are sponges. They are continuously in developmental periods where they are heavily and easily influenced. They find people to look up to and model themselves after. They search for people to follow—in life, on social media, in the media. Yet, we control the gate. We are a major filter in their search results. So we need to ask ourselves, "Who do I want my kids to follow and have influence in their lives?"

GOOD COMPANY / BAD COMPANY

"Bad company corrupts good morals" (1 Cor. 15:33). Five little words that mean so much. When Jesus entered Jairus' home, He kicked out the bad company. It was that important to Him, and it was that important for the well-being of the girl.

Let's address the devil-shaped elephant in the room here, "Didn't Jesus say we are to try to teach others about Him?" you might ask. The quick answer to that is, well, yes. Teaching people about Jesus and allowing them personal access into our home are two different things.

Here's one way to see this in action. Jesus often sent out His disciples to neighboring towns on mission. However, it seems as though He didn't send them alone but in pairs or groups. They also had a plan to return together. So, when going out to teach people about Jesus, they strived to influence others while being careful not to allow others to influence them negatively. The time spent *out* was monitored. The people who came *in* were filtered.

As parents, we want our kids to grow up with positive influences in their lives. We can look around this world and see all the bad company that can corrupt the morals we are trying to instill in them. So, as gatekeepers, we have the responsibility and the authority to limit who comes into their lives while teaching them to reach out at the appropriate time. But, like I said, we are not the only people our kids will glean from. Caring adults outside of parents can have a great deal of influence. Which begs the question, "Who else is influencing our kids?"

Having worked as a middle school counselor as well as having coached a number of sports, I've witnessed the influence adults have on kids each day in public schools. When we send our kids off to school, a team, a club, or any activity where adults are leading, we are entrusting the adults involved to make a positive impact on our kids. I bet if you think back to your childhood, you can probably picture a few adults who made a great impact on your own life. God-willing, our kids will look back in twenty to thirty years and reflect on a few trusted individuals as well.

Having worked in public education, I am a fan of the role educators play in our kids' lives. Our girls all attend public schools, and I believe they receive a great education from wonderful people who care deeply. They are learning from people who teach them not only educational material but also soft skills like communication, empathy, organization, problem-solving, teamwork, time management, and more. What they may or may not be learning is centering their compass on Jesus.

While it's important to consider who is influencing our kids, it's vital that we understand who is modeling their lifestyle after Jesus and pointing our kids toward Him.

I am biased when I say this, but I believe some of the greatest weapons Jesus has put on this planet are children and student ministry leaders. Not the paid staff but the volunteers who spend time with our kids and teens week in and week out. I watch my kids get excited about seeing them. They talk about them with admiration. After spending time on weekend retreats, my girls would giggle, telling us stories of them singing together and just being silly. The relationships they form over those silly moments often give them the credibility to have deeper conversations about Jesus in their lives. Their leaders will send them messages wishing them luck on the first day of school, letting them know they are praying for them. They show up at events and performances our girls are in. These leaders are living lives chasing Jesus and influencing our kids in their own walk with

Jesus. It is extremely valuable to have people set an example of godly living for our kids who aren't mom and dad.

Tiffani has spent time in this role, leading a group of girls. From middle school up, she watched them graduate high school. I know of the fun times they had together. And of the seemingly meaningless conversations they had during those younger years. I know when they were in high school, the girls would tell my wife things they would not tell their parents. I know they asked her for advice when it came to friendships and dating.

I want our girls to have women in their lives like Tiffani. Women outside of our home who are following Jesus, who our girls can call and talk with when they do not want to talk to us. Jesus brought Peter, James, and John into Jairus' home. I want to bring leaders like them into my home to impact my daughters. If bad company corrupts good morals, I want to surround my girls with good company to influence godly living.

For some, it will be youth leaders influencing their kids. For others, it may be grandparents, aunts or uncles, a neighbor, or that teacher or coach you know is walking with Jesus. No matter who you "bring into your home" to influence your kids, our parameters should be someone who is chasing Jesus with all their heart, soul, mind, and strength.

The flip side of this is that we need to keep the gate closed to some of the people in our kids' lives. Remember, we are responsible for monitoring the potential negative impact some people can have on our kids. Adults who do not share the same moral framework can also influence our children in a direction we are not in favor of. Too often, we hear others suggest that we are too strict as parents. One of my wife's friends has suggested that we are raising naïve girls and that we will do more harm than good by not letting them understand what the "real world" is all about. Did I mention this friend doesn't share our family values? I am alright with my kids being naïve until they reach an age where they can understand and comprehend right from wrong.

Pulling the gate tight can get difficult when it comes to family, friends, and neighbors. But, if we follow the same principle Jesus laid out for His disciples—go out in the world and influence others, then return to your gated community—we will experience a healthy dose of family, friends, and neighbors we can spend time with who are not chasing Jesus. This doesn't mean we have to ex-communicate them from our lives. It may mean, however, that they are not the ones spending the most time with our kids.

Navigating who our kids spend time with and look up to is tricky but greatly important. The adults in their lives are influential and will either influence them towards God or away from Him.

THE FIVE

There is a long-standing theory that goes something like, "If you want to know your future, take a look at the five people you spend the most time with because you will become the average of their make-up." This concept has been utilized in business and career development. Yet, I believe it has so many connections within our personal and spiritual lives as well. If we want to follow God more closely or become more intentional parents, we can look at the five people we spend the most time with and discern how this group is challenging us to grow in our faith and as parents.

It also works with our kids, don't you think? If we want to see a glimpse into their future, we can look at the peers they choose to spend the most time with. Do you know who their friends are? They're going to play a huge role in your kids' development. Peers become increasingly more influential in their lives as they progress through elementary, middle, and all the way through high school.

Starting young, we have the opportunity to support play dates with our kids and their friends. At this stage, it is completely on us to regulate who they spend time with. As they grow through elementary school, they develop friendships in school and in activities. We still have the ability to foster time outside of these spaces with kids we believe would be a good fit for them and for our values. But this process only becomes more challenging the older they get. Yet the way we structure it early in their childhood will play a role in allowing us to continue to have a voice in their friendships as they grow up.

I cannot overstate the influence our kids' peers have on them. Over and over again, working as a middle school counselor, I met with parents who were concerned when their kids switched friend groups. It was especially concerning for the parents when the new group seemed to be different from the last group. When this new group of friends had a reputation for disrespecting authority and messing with alcohol and drugs, parents would ask if I could talk with their child about these newfound friends. The conversations went like clockwork. I would point out that I am aware of the group's reputation for risky behavior. The predictable response would be something like, "They may do those things, but I don't." To which I would say, "You may not be now, but you will. It's only a matter of time." Often, the students would argue that they like these friends but don't feel pressured to do any of the bad stuff. The reality, of course, was that if these students continued to hang out with their new group, it was only a matter of time before they would take on the behaviors of the group. They would conform to the norm of the group. Peer influence is a powerful thing.

If you're in a season of watching your kids switch groups, flirt with values that aren't God-honoring, or are feeling discouraged, just remember, your influence can go a long way.

Even as they grow, we can nudge them toward friends and relationships that we believe will have a positive impact. If our kids attend public school, we may not see who they talk and play with. That said, we can take time and intentionally work to understand who they spend time with, what they're like, and what they talk and laugh about. Of course, the more we engage in healthy gatekeeping in their younger years, the more influence we'll have to speak into this as they grow. Nonetheless, we also have control and influence over who they spend time with outside of school. We can encourage friendships we believe are positive while limiting those that may pull them towards things we wouldn't support.

We shape our kids through who we are and how we teach them. How we live and how we pass it on. And we help shape them by who we allow them to spend time with. Until they're out and on their own, we have the ability to open and close the gate to friends coming in and out of their lives.

WHAT GOES IN, MUST COME OUT

I have the spiritual gift of taking almost any phrase someone says and breaking into an aptly themed song. One of my girls was talking about shaving. Without hesitation, I immediately jumped into an old country song about shaving. My daughter, obviously a gifted individual herself, joined me in singing the song. After a bit, I paused and said, "Wait, when did you ever hear that song?"

She replied, "I don't know, I think just from hearing you sing it." It hit me. Even though in those outbursts it was never a conscious thought of what I would break into, she was hearing it and picking it up. Our kids, like you and me, are constantly taking in information from all over. And what we take in, ultimately, comes out.

Whether it is our singing, the shows on TV, the music they listen to, or what they consume through social media, all of it is absorbed into not just their minds but also their hearts. What we allow in will manifest in our thoughts, feelings, and behaviors. Jesus told us about this in Luke 6:45, saying, "The good man out of the good treasure of his heart brings forth what is good; and the evil man out of the evil treasure brings forth what is evil; for his mouth speaks from that which fills his heart." It's wild to stop and consider this, isn't it? We are constantly taking in information, and as we do, it becomes the treasure of our hearts and minds. Out of that treasure, our hearts speak.

We are the gatekeepers of what buries itself in our kids' hearts and minds. Which means we will see what goes in by what comes out of their mouths.

As our kids hit middle school, the books they were exposed to were quite different than those we saw come home in elementary school. As we would read the back covers, then bits and pieces throughout the text, we often found ourselves questioning whether or not these books were good for our kids to read. The response, "Well, I got it from my teacher's library, so it must be okay," was quickly found to not be a valid argument in our home. Now, as I noted at the start of this discussion, we may err on the side of being overprotective parents, but we also understand the impact of the information they take in. All things are allowable, but not all things are beneficial (1 Corinthians 10:23). The books they have access to may be allowed by their schools, but they're not all beneficial to be taking in. This was not something Tiffani and I knew we would have to deal with, however, it falls within our roles as the gatekeepers of our kids' lives. There are a lot of book options, thousands they could freely choose from, but they would need to fall within our level of acceptability.

What we read shapes us in the same way that what we hear impacts us. The radio in our vehicles is often turned to Christian radio. I want our kids to have the truths of God's Word singing through their minds. We were at a Christian concert a few years back where Casting Crowns headlined one of the evenings. During the day they were interviewed so we walked over to listen in for a bit. At one point, they were asked how they came up with the lyrics for their songs. I remember the answer. They talked about how important Scripture is in their music because, as they stated, when people leave church, they're not humming the pastor's sermon, but they could be humming their song. In a humble way, they understood the weight of music.

Songs easily get stuck in our heads. I understand this. I hear a word, and I'm instantly singing a song with that word in it. What songs will you be singing when you are prompted? For me, I want the majority to be Christian songs. I want my kids to be singing Christian songs that remind them of His Truths. In order to have those songs imprinted in their minds, they have to hear them more often than on Sunday morning. So, nearly all we play in our vehicles and in our home mimic what we might hear when gathered with the Church. As a consequence, I have a hard time telling them to be quiet when they are belting out songs praising Jesus! Usually, I just smile and give thanks.

The songs we sing become the truths we live by. There is plenty of music in this world that is not edifying to anyone. We don't have to dig very deep to find music that would lead our kids to believe everyone is drinking, doing drugs, and having sex. Those are not the lyrics I want playing in their minds as they're walking into school. We are the gatekeepers.

This goes for TV as well. The TV is not on a lot in our house, but when it is, it is governed. Most of us gravitate toward the norm, and what we see and hear most often is normalized. "Everybody is doing it" becomes the value we will move toward. During our kid's earlier stages of development, if we allow the TV to influence them, ultimately defining what is normal in this world, they will come to an understanding that does not jive with Jesus' plan for how we are to live our lives.

You and I both know that our kids will be introduced to things that are certainly not biblical. This is not news to us. Any of us. Yet, being introduced to something and growing up to believe it is normal are two different things.

Our kids will be exposed to all sorts of sins in this world. If they read books with sexual content in them, if we allow (and thus approve) of them watching TV that includes normalizing one-night stands, living together prior to marriage, and all other aspects of worldly living, they will grow up with the idea that this is not only normal but a path they could travel as well. On the contrary, if they grow up not seeing these lifestyles as normal and right, when they hear and see things that don't seem to align with God's Word, it will strike them as odd. Something about the language, actions, and beliefs expressed as normal will not sit well in their hearts and minds. That's where you and I, their parents, come in. We have the opportunity to talk through these challenging ideas and help guide them toward Jesus' path.

No. Our goal isn't to completely shelter our kids from the "real world," as Tiffani's friend said, but to limit exposure to things that are of the world while we're here in it. Didn't Jesus say that even though we need to live in this world, we are not to be of it (John 17:14-16)? We cannot escape the sin around us, but we do not have to live as if we are part of it. He has a different path for us. He has a better path for us. He modeled that we are to watch who and what we allow into our homes and into our eyes and ears. We are the gatekeepers.

CONCLUSION

Jesus taught Jairus, along with each one of us, an important lesson in how to manage our homes. Keep those who foster a bad influence on our kids out while welcoming those who believe in Jesus into our homes. We want to surround ourselves and our kids with positive role models. We know people influence us—for good or bad. Even as adults. We also know the things we allow into our minds impact us—especially our kids.

It is difficult to say "No" to our kids, isn't it? They are often good at rationalizing, presenting a good case, and begging to do things we don't want them to do. And deep down, we want them to like us. So, we want to say "Yes" to them whenever possible because it makes them happy and it temporarily enables us to feel good about our relationship. It is not fun for them to be mad at us for not allowing them to do something we don't think is right, good, or safe. It's not fun for us either. The easy thing would be to give in and give them what they want. But the easy thing isn't always the right thing. We are better off being their parent than their friend. We are better off being respected than walked over. We are better off being the gatekeeper than the open door.

CENTERING 🏠 JESUS

As gatekeepers, we control who and what impacts our kids. It's our job. If we limit who comes into our kids' lives, sure, we may take flack for it. And if we limit what we allow our kids to watch, listen to, or read, we will probably take heat for it as well. And yes, our kids may get upset with our decisions. So might extended family members and friends. The good news is we don't have to stand before them at the end of our lives and justify our decisions. We will, however, stand before Jesus, the eternal gatekeeper. The one who modeled the way for us. He showed us what it is like to limit who and what comes into our homes. Now, it is up to us to act. Who will we surround our kids with? What will we surround our kids with?

4 REFLECTION QUESTIONS

1. How do you set the standards for what enters your kids' eyes and ears within your home? What do you allow and not allow them to read, listen to, and watch? Why?

2. As you assess what enters your kids' minds and ears, are there boundaries you're discovering that need clarifying?

3. Do your children have adult mentors in their lives? If not, who do you know that loves Jesus and models Christlikeness that you might consider as a potential mentor for them?

4. What challenges do you face being the gatekeeper for your children? How will you overcome those challenges as you strive to put Jesus at the center of your home?

5 You Can Do It Different

From little on, my kids were in love with all things Disney. It didn't take long for our little girls to start dressing up and playing princess. As the years kept coming, in our home, that meant the girls kept coming. One, then another, and another, and so on. As I write, we have five girls. When they were young, playing princess, dressing up, and watching Disney movies, we dreamt of taking our girls to experience Disney World. We longed to have them continue their imaginative play and experience characters and rides and the magic of what happens when a young child steps into such an immersive theme park. We were warned of the costs, of course, yet it seemed like such a great opportunity to bond as a family.

So, we started planning. As birthdays and Christmases piled up, we stashed money away into a separate account labeled "Disney Fund." We knew they didn't need to add more toys on these special holidays as family members blessed them with more than they could even use. Instead, our presents would be delayed, rolled into a family trip at some point as the money added up and the adventure paid for.

As the money slowly gathered, Jesus slowly worked on our hearts. We strived to put Him at the center of our family. Yet, as the deposits continued, we asked ourselves, "How is this trip going to help us put Jesus at the center of our family?"

I imagined bringing my kids to one of the fabulous theme parks, hoping to see their eyes light up with utter joy. I imagined how much fun we would have going on rides, meeting characters, and taking family photos to lock in the memories. Then, I started to think of the memories that would last. And as much fun as it would be, I couldn't shake the feeling that it would feel empty after returning home. What would we gain from spending that kind of money on a trip chasing a fantasy? Would it help our family live on mission for Jesus?

Tiffani and I decided to rename that fund "Family Mission Fund." We still wanted an adventure, it's just that we wanted them to meet people, not characters. I want to take pictures to remember how God impacted them. I wanted to see them light up, finding joy in our Savior. We longed for this sort of family experience. To go on a trip where our kids' eyes would be opened wide to how big our God is. No doubt Disney would serve up a world of enchantment, but honestly, we longed to serve others, not to be served.

My hope was that we would experience a trip where we grew in our faith together, striving to put Jesus at the center of our family. We just didn't believe that would be achieved in a theme park. Now, I have nothing against Disney World. I have nothing against those who take it all in and make memories with their families. We just had a different desire. One placed on our hearts that we couldn't shake. We wanted our kids to meet others from a different culture, in a different country, who lived a different way of life. I longed for them to see how God works in others' lives, even if those lives are vastly different than our own.

Fortunately, through our church, we have ministry partners in different countries. These missionaries get to serve people with cultures and backgrounds much different than our own. Our kids had heard stories but had yet to see such a distinctly different culture face-to-face.

For years, we have been sponsoring a child. Personally, I have had the opportunity to meet her on a couple occasions while leading overseas missions trips through our church. I wanted that experience for my kids. I wanted them to witness God at work, not just in our home or in our city, but all over the world. That He is at work in villages where the average home could fit within our living room. He is at work in towns where the water is undrinkable. I wanted them to see how circumstances don't have to affect their joy. I wanted my girls to see that our God not only loves us but that He loves His people worldwide.

After years of saving, it happened. Tiffani and I were able to cash-in our Family Mission Fund and take all seven of us to Panama. It is a trip sealed in all of our hearts. We were able to experience being a family on mission, and I'll never forget it.

We experienced cultural differences, language barriers, and God at work. We viewed the world through a different lens. I think it's safe to say that we saw things, in some ways, as God sees them. We saw life through the eyes of orphans, scarcity, and desire. We saw life through the eyes of love, plenty, and contentment. Smiles and play can overcome language barriers. People with less often have more. My girls saw that school in Panama had similarities and differences to their own experiences. Church looked a little different, but we worshiped the same God. After eleven days in Panama, I don't think anyone wanted to leave. To this day, our girls long for a return trip.

Looking back, I knew that I wanted them to experience a different lifestyle in hopes of seeing God in a different light. I wanted them to live differently, if only for the length of a trip, in hopes of our family choosing to live differently upon return. I don't want to chase the American dream. I don't want my kids to chase the American dream. I want us to be like Jairus and chase after Jesus. For us, this meant transforming our Disney Fund into a Family Mission Fund. It's a subtle change that, I believe, can help each one of our families put Jesus at the center.

LISTEN TO JESUS

If we are going to parent differently than the world would have us, we need to listen to Jesus. Jesus gave Jairus and his wife orders to feed their daughter. Although the story doesn't follow up with whether or not they listened to Jesus, I get the impression that after witnessing Jesus raise her from the dead, they would have followed through with anything He suggested. Feeding her, of all things, seems quite an easy task considering the circumstances. So long as they could even move from being in absolute awe after what just happened to their daughter.

Jairus watched his daughter go from breathless to full of life. He watched the miraculous happen before his eyes. I'm comfortable concluding that he would listen and act accordingly to Jesus' follow-up instructions to feed his daughter.

If it were me, I'd open the fridge and ask for specifics. "What should I feed her? What's a good meal after rising from the dead?" I would run to the store, go for takeout, or even pretend I could cook if that were asked of me. I imagine they would follow anything He said after Jesus revived their little girl. In light of all this, we have to ask ourselves a simple question. "Do we follow what Jesus says after He saves our children? After He saves us?"

You can imagine Jairus asking Jesus to stay. They would offer to make dinner, pull up a couple chairs, invite Him and His disciples to stay the night and pull out all the stops so Jesus could stay as long as He would like.

Just think of all the questions Jairus would want to ask Jesus while he had the opportunity. Once Jesus entered Jairus' home, I can't imagine he would ever want Jesus to leave. Would you? Again, the man witnessed his daughter go from dead to fully alive.

Witnessing a child go from dead to alive is likely to make anyone, I would think, want to obey all Jesus says. And while He has taught us many things through His Word, it's important to view them through a particular lens. There's a point of reference repeated in Scripture, and stated by Jesus, that is intended to help us get our bearings when choosing whether or not to obey His commands, and that is that we are to live in this world, remembering that we aren't of this world (John 17:13-16). We live here temporarily, but that does not mean we are to follow what the "world" has to offer.

We will be challenged, if not pressured, to adhere to the world's standards for raising our kids. We are expected to raise our kids differently. And you know what? We will feel like outcasts. We will be the odd ones out at times. That's exactly what Jesus asks us to do—live in this world and be different. When we seek to follow Jesus' plan for our lives and for the lives of our kids, it means we listen to what He has to say. As a result, we feed our kids differently than others—not literally but biblically speaking—which means we won't feed them a diet of contemporary culture.

There's nothing so contemporary as modern technology, which endlessly connects us to the world in every facet of life. And if you're like most parents, you've been tempted to give in to the staunch requests of your kids to have endless access. After all, technology is their first language. They understand it from the womb on. As their friends get to utilize technology at early ages, will our kids?

And don't even get me started on dating. Dating is a common thing in kids' lives. I watched it unfold as a middle school counselor and continue to hear about it from my elementary and middle school kids. Many think it's just a natural part of growing up. Like puppy-love. Will we follow the natural contemporary course or hold a different line? These are just a couple of the challenges we will face in raising our kids differently. I haven't even touched on clothing choices, social media, chores, or politics! At the end of the day, will we listen to Jesus' instructions on how to feed them, or will we listen to someone else to direct us?

What Jesus did for Jairus' child, He can do for ours. Jesus wants to enter into our homes and bring our children from spiritual death to fully alive. And you know what? He wants to stay and remain the focal point we build our lives around.

WORLDLY DEMANDS

We have great intentions, don't we? I know you want what is best for your kids. So do I. And on our best days, we can believe the best thing for them is Jesus. Then life happens, and we get inundated and overwhelmed with all the options and events our kids have going on. Instead of pausing, looking to and speaking with Jesus, then adjusting course, we get on the treadmill and guess what? It just keeps moving, often pulling us further away from Jesus.

Tiffani and I had always vowed to be different. We strive to be different. We want to put Jesus and keep Jesus at the center of our home. But life, well, life happens. I have found that if we do not diligently challenge the status quo and constantly fight to keep Jesus where He belongs, it is so easy to watch all outside events and opportunities make headway into our home.

One of the areas worth fighting for, one that we discovered early on, was that family time is a priceless commodity. Tiffani and I try to guard the time we have together as a family, but I admit it's an imperfect process. In fact, I'm currently writing this on an evening where our five girls are each involved in some sort of extracurricular activity with three different drop-off and pick-up times. What's more, we hurried home in order to eat a rushed dinner and get everyone packed up and ready to go just so we could hurry back out the door. But that was just the beginning. Once we're done with all the practices, we'll have just enough time to go home and climb into bed. It is safe to say we have found ourselves on the treadmill—even as we have been fighting against it.

We often say Jesus is the priority in our home, but is He?

On nights like this, it is hard to believe that we are doing it right. The battle rages on. I want my kids to have opportunities to explore sports and the arts. But I'm left asking myself, "What is a good balance?" If left up to chance, our kids will be pushed, pulled, and persuaded to be involved in every opportunity that exists. They all sound so great! But how much is too much?

As a Christ follower and someone who works in the church, I believe in the value and absolute necessity of being present in regular worship services. For us, this means Sundays, and for our teens, Wednesday evenings. Years past, community-wide, Sundays and Wednesday evenings were sacred. Culturally, they were relatively off-limits from activities that would steal people away from engaging in local church services. Schools blocked them off to protect family faith time from extracurricular activities and sports practice. Yet, today, Sundays and Wednesdays are no longer viewed as different. They're simply another day of the week on the calendar.

We bumped into this reality when Brinley informed us there was a middle school orchestra concert scheduled for a Wednesday night. In our home, Wednesdays are set aside for youth group. We didn't realize this would have to be a conversation. Or that a decision about how we want to view Wednesdays would need to be made. So, Tiffani and I discussed it first. Then, we invited Brinley to share her thoughts. I simply opened the conversation with her by saying, "Your concert is scheduled for a Wednesday night. What do you think about that?" Her response made things easy. "Wednesdays are youth group nights. I'm not missing youth group." And, with her thumbs up, I emailed her teacher to let him know. The whole event went smoother than I had anticipated. Why? In part because of her reaction. And her reaction wasn't flippant, it was the overflow of our faith-filled values having been practiced in real time together.

Can I vent a little here? It is frustrating to watch friends having to choose between their kids' activities and engaging in weekly life with the local church. I am growing increasingly frustrated with activities being scheduled on Sunday mornings.

When a gymnastics meet was scheduled for a Sunday, the conversation proved a little more challenging than our Wednesday night orchestra conflict had been. For gymnastics, our girls are registered for weekend meets months in advance. However, upon registering, we don't know if they will compete on Saturday or Sunday until just a couple weeks prior. Crazy, right? For people who like to plan ahead, this was a new challenge. There we were, holding their first meet schedule during their first competitive gymnastics season, and sure enough, they were scheduled for a Sunday morning competition.

When I mentioned to Cambria and Lily that their meet was scheduled for Sunday morning, I wasn't met with a shared frustration. They weren't as bothered by the thought of missing church on Sunday for a big meet. What's more, they quickly offered a compromise: they would watch the service online on their way to the meet. As much as I am grateful for the ability to livestream church services, nothing compares to being in the same room with the rest of our church family. I was not immediately won over by this compromise. So, Tiffani and I talked about it behind closed doors. We knew we would be setting the standard for years to come. That's not to say we wouldn't be able to make a course correction, only that the first response would be important.

We value church. We value relationships. We value putting Jesus at the center of our home. For the most part, our kids value those things too. But they also value gymnastics and had been looking forward to competing for years. There we were, on the cusp of their first competition, and we had to make a choice to either let them do something they love, knowing there are fifty-one other Sundays in the year or draw a hard line and show our values in action, putting Jesus in the place He deserves?

We made what we believed was a solid compromise. You see, the meet was a couple-hour drive from our home, which was why they could not attend a service as usual and make it to the meet in time. There is, however, a church in the city where their meet was located connected to our church's denomination. Even better, we have friends who attend that church. My wife and girls would be able to get up early, drive to that church, and attend service with them, then make the quick drive to the competition with time to spare. All parties agreed that this option kept our value of attending the local church on Sundays while still allowing Cambria and Lily to compete in their meet.

This won't be the last time we have to figure out how we hold true to our values in a world where we are bombarded by endless options and pulled in so many directions. I realize that you may have read through our decision-making process and where we landed as a family and concluded that we're off the mark. For you, our reactions to these situations may have been too weak. For others, we may have come across too heavy-handed. Sure, we may need course corrections along the way, and I have no doubt we will be challenged over and over again to hold to our values on Wednesdays, Sundays, and every other day of the week. Regardless, we entered into these decisions with the knowledge that we want to live differently than the world wants us to live. While we may not get it right every time, I'm confident that by processing together as a family with clear values before us, we'll continue to run after Jesus each step of the way.

Putting Jesus at the center of our home and listening to what He wants for us is easier said than done, don't you think? It doesn't take long for days, weeks, or months to pass before we look back and think, "How did we get so off course?" Putting Jesus at the center of our home is an ongoing task. It is a never-ending goal we will continue to strive toward.

BOUNDARIES

In today's world, not only is our time being challenged by all sorts of activities, but our time is easily consumed. A major source of consumption happens to be a device that's either in our faces or against our ears. Of course, you know what I'm talking about— these small computers, kindly referred to as phones, seem to take up a huge amount of our focus. And not just in regard to our kids either.

It didn't take long to realize our little ones, even before being able to walk, were mesmerized by our addictive devices. As parents, it's a simple solution to hand a baby our phone and watch them be entertained for long periods. For many of us, as our kids have grown, technology has become their first babysitter. Maybe it was a TV, but odds are, your interactive tablet or phone did a much better job.

It's no longer unusual for kids to sport their own phones before even graduating from elementary school. For those parents who either haven't given in yet or who have plans to wait, our kids will feel the constant pressure to want to fit in and to have a phone like "everyone else."

Jesus didn't say much about cell phone use. However, He did speak on many other areas of Christian living we can glean from.

Over the years, I have had the opportunity to speak with teens at our church about idols. As we talk about honoring God above all things, we usually begin by discussing what things we tend to put above Him. For the students who struggle to come up with their own list, I usually pose a question like, "If I were to take something of yours away from you, how upset would you be about it? If it would be devastating, that might be an indication that the item is an idol." Those who have phones often quickly acknowledge they would be pretty upset if they lost them.

Often, on mission trips or weekend retreats, we do not allow phones or other technology. It can be a deal breaker as soon as some students find this out. They will not attend a weekend retreat if they cannot have their phones by their side. These devices are addicting. I have also witnessed the reverse. I've watched students who reluctantly left their phones behind wrap up their time away, grateful they were able to disconnect from their devices and reconnect with people. My point is that we will be tempted to give in to our kids' desires for a phone before they are disciplined enough to handle one. Not only will they be faced with addictive tendencies, but they'll be subjected to social media platforms, text groups, and other means capable of introducing or exposing them to mature content.

I have talked with too many parents whose kids have been exposed to things they wish they had not seen. I have talked with too many parents horrified to see the pictures their kids took of themselves and sent to others. I have talked with too many parents whose kids naïvey started talking to someone they believed to be a new friend, only to find out the person on the other side of the conversation was not who they said they were.

While all of that is a modern reality associated with giving our kids access to the world via handheld computers, not everything associated with having a phone is bad. To be fair, phones are neither good nor bad. Like any tool, they can be beneficial. They can also be damaging. If we hold off until our kids are more mature and able to handle the challenges that come with having a personal device, no doubt we will be going against the norms of our culture. Yes, our kids may feel left out. And yes, you and I may feel like we are mean parents, prudes, or the odd ones out.

And you know what? That's alright. Be different. We don't have to give in to social pressures. In fact, if we follow Jesus, we will have to get comfortable with going against the grain.

In our house, we have tried a number of ways to be different throughout the years. All with the purpose of putting Jesus at the center. Currently, we have an odd day each week called "No Technology Tuesday" when we ban the use of technology: TV, computers, phones, etc. Now, we are not so stubborn that our kids can't do homework on their computers if required. Generally, though, most things are off, and instead, we promote talking, playing games, or being active together. In part, this day is set aside to help us manage our dependence on devices. But it's also intended to help us focus on one another without distraction.

"When will the Schley kids get their own phones?" Great question. No clue. Not yet. We did, however, compromise and purchased a home phone. No. Not one of those old rotary dials hanging on our wall with an extended, curly cable. A home cell phone. Generally speaking, it stays at home. It is not their phone. It is ours. When my wife and I are both away, and the kids are home alone, they can reach us. It provides us comfort knowing we can be in touch with them. That is the purpose of the phone. That said, my girls have taken the phone to different events or places where we believe it would be beneficial. It's a work in progress. So far, this sort of *different* works for us, but we are always open to tweaking our rules and strategies.

And then there's dating. Dating is a whole other topic where we are seemingly different from the norm. It is another area where we, as parents, need to establish clear boundaries for our kids. Like most parents, we encourage our girls to have friends. Dating, however, is not something we encourage. In fact, we have a simple house rule when it comes to our girls dating. When they turn sixteen, they can start to date if they so choose.

Looking through Scripture, I keep coming back to the strict purpose of dating—to get married. Dating is meant to determine if a couple is compatible for marriage. The question I pose to teens is, "Are you ready to get married?" If the answer is no, which it almost always is, I ask, "Then why would you date?" The conversation always expands from there, but it is a necessary starting point in order to help them understand the weight of their actions and desires.

Our kids will often come home and talk about their friends "dating" other people. Elementary school dating is drama-filled fun! For our girls, my hope is that they remain free from immature drama while they're young while setting them up to be free from unnecessary heartache as they go through middle and high school. I'm sure they will hear about it from friends, even being challenged and enticed by it. But I'm also confident I can handle the accusations of deprivation. After all, I'd rather have them blame me and not face heartache than face unnecessary heartache, or worse, in order to fit within the world's standards. Together, we'll be seen as different. But in case you've missed the ongoing point of this chapter, if we aren't raising our kids differently compared to today's standards, we aren't doing it right. If we aren't feeding them a different, Christ-centered diet, then we aren't following Jesus.

CONCLUSION

Jesus made a simple request of Jairus and his wife. They were to feed their daughter. There is such simplicity in this idea, yet so much depth and truth.

Jesus made multiple mentions about eating throughout the Scriptures. Food would supply an immediate physical need, but those who would eat it would be hungry again and again. What He was offering was so much greater. In John 6:26-40, when the crowds came after Jesus, He confronted them about the real reason they followed Him. Jesus told them they were simply following Him because He had fed them bread. He was saying that if they looked past the Giver of bread to the food itself, well, they were missing the most important thing. They were so focused on the bread of this life that they were in danger of missing the Author of eternal life.

Don't put this life above the next.

Don't be so caught up in the here and now that you lose focus on the ultimate prize. Guard your goals. If we are not careful, we'll think our earthly hunger can satisfy us with the temporary meals the world offers, only to walk right past the most important feast right in front of us. A feast designed to quench our spiritual hunger.

The challenging part of this life is that the longer we go without physical bread, the more we crave it and will do anything for it. On the other hand, the longer we go without being filled spiritually, the less we hunger for it. Jairus heard Jesus tell him to feed his daughter. The request seemed simple. Give her something to eat. Get her some bread. What bread would Jairus feed his daughter? What bread would Jairus feed *His* daughter?

If Jairus solely focused on feeding his daughter bread, he would run the risk of missing what Jesus offered his family. Why? Because Jesus offers something beyond our stomachs. Jesus offers something different.

When we follow Jesus in this way, we will be different. He knows this. He warned us of this. Jesus told His disciples that if they were of the world, they would be loved by the world (John 15:19). The thing is, they were not of the world. Neither are we. Which means we can anticipate people not understanding why we do what we do. People will disagree with us. Our kids might even fight against the boundaries we set. Set them anyway.

If we are going to be parents who follow Jesus, we are going to have to be different. When this world is focused on feeding kids the bread of this life, we will be focused on feeding them the bread of eternal life.

5 REFLECTION QUESTIONS

1. How would you describe the differences between parenting according to the Bible and parenting according to the world?

2. If you were to have a conversation with Jesus about parenting, what do you think He might say to you? In what areas would He challenge, encourage, and compliment you?

3. How do you balance living in the world but not being of the world? What worldly pressures are you currently facing? How will you face them with a biblical mindset?

4. With all the good opportunities for your kids to get involved in, what boundaries have you established in your home to determine what they can say yes to? How do you handle practices, games, and other activities scheduled on Sundays?

5. What boundaries do you have regarding things like phones and dating? What parameters and expectations do you and your spouse need to gain clarity and unity?

6   What Do I Do Now

December 29th, 2022 will forever be etched into my memories. The day started on a beach and ended in a hospital room. Our Lily had been sick for several weeks. We took her to see her doctor as she had just seemed a little lethargic and not her normal, spunky self. Something was off. Her doctor thought she was recovering from a virus she had a few weeks prior. "Give it a couple more weeks," he thought, "and it should run its course. If she doesn't get better, come back, and we'll do a deeper dive." That all seemed to make sense. Until she didn't get better.

We left the cold and snowy Wisconsin weather for the sunshine in Florida for Christmas break. When we arrived to visit with family and friends, Lily was still not herself which became undeniably clear when we went to a pool and she lay on a lounger. "I just want to sunbathe," she said. Meanwhile, her sisters and friends were having a great time in the pool. This wasn't her. When we went to the beach, it was more of the same. The girl who is usually running, splashing, cartwheeling, and building sand castles, was lying on a towel, looking pale.

It was a friend who asked the question I can still hear today. "Did you consider diabetes?" Tiffani replied, "Did you know that runs in Brian's family?" It checked all the boxes. Looking back, she had been drinking more water and making more trips to the restroom. Her lethargy fit the symptoms. Tiffani called our doctor back home and let him know she had not gotten better, and so, given the current symptoms, we asked about diabetes. "What should we do?" she asked. "Go get tested there. Don't come home before you get her checked out."

Leaving the beach, we dropped our daughters off with friends, then Tiffani, Lily, and I took a trip to the emergency room. We were quickly seen by a wonderful crew and explained a bit of the history. "So, we are wondering if we could rule out diabetes first?" The nurse practitioner agreed, suggesting we do that right away. Without hesitation, another nurse retrieved a machine to check Lily's blood sugar levels. The nurse poked Lily's finger, put a drop of her blood onto the machine, and within seconds said, "Five hundred forty-nine." I was floored and quickly asked, "Did you say five forty-nine?" I knew what that meant. A typical blood sugar level is 70-110. Tiffani looked at me and asked, "What does that mean?" "It means our suspicion is correct," I said.

Wanting to be positive about the outcome of the test, I asked our nurse if we could verify her blood sugar level with another machine. She knew the life change this number meant and sensed my trepidation. She agreed and left the room for another machine. This time, it read 529. Deep breath. I smiled at Lily to give her some reassurance. She is an observant girl and was reading the room, wondering what it all meant. In her nine-year-old ability to process information she had never heard before, she calmly asked, "Am I going to die?" I replied, "No, baby, it's nothing like that. This just means we will be staying at the hospital a couple days. They'll get you feeling better, and then we will head home with some medicine."

Lily was quickly moved to a room where they initiated a couple IVs in order to bring her blood sugar levels down. After about six hours, she took an ambulance ride to a children's hospital. The ambulance ride was the highlight of Lily's day! When she heard she would get to ride in an ambulance, she was pretty excited, though, by that time, she was also ready for bed.

With the emergency passed, Tiffani and I now had to process how to proceed. We had four kids staying with phenomenal friends during our trip to the ER. "You do whatever you need to do. We have your kids taken care of," they said, offering to watch the kids as needed over the coming days.

With the girls taken care of, we prepared to leave for the ambulance ride. One of us could go in the ambulance with Lily; the other could follow behind.

"I'm not leaving my baby!" Tiffani assured me. "Well, alrighty then. I guess we have made our decision." This wasn't a surprise to me. I had already planned for it, considering I wouldn't dare suggest Tiffani leave our daughter's side in that moment. To be honest, I'm glad that was her response. I want that to be her response. She is the mother. A great mother. That's always been her role, and I wouldn't have it any other way.

The only question left was, "What's my role in this moment?"

My role was to go be with our other four girls. They love their sister, Lily. We had been able to call and message them throughout the day to keep them updated, but they were still certainly worried for her. I wanted to be with them. I wanted to calm their nerves and let them know their sister would be okay. As Lily and Tiffani entered the ambulance, I gave them hugs and kisses, then immediately went to our friend's home to do the same with our other four girls. They had a ton of questions, and thankfully, I was able to answer most of them. They had also made cards for Lily. Their cards were so sweet, kind, and thoughtful that they caused the emotional weight of the day to finally catch up with me. Reading their words melted my heart, which overflowed down my face.

I was able to give those cards to Lily the next morning as I drove to be with her and Tiffani in the intensive care unit. And for the next few days, I would drive to be with Lily in the morning, leaving her at bedtime to put our other four girls to bed after having spent the day with our friends. That was my role. Tiffani stayed with Lily. She never left her side. That was her role.

JAIRUS AND HIS WIFE

Jairus knew his role. The moment he realized he needed help, he left his daughter and wife at home and went in search of Jesus. I imagine he saw his daughter's health deteriorating. He saw the fear in his wife's eyes. Jairus knew he had to do something, anything to try to help his baby girl. They had already tried everything they knew, yet nothing was working. She rested, she ate what she could, and the local doctor checked on her without a feasible cure. Still, she continued to weaken. Her skin grew clammy and pale. Like any father reaching for an answer, he stopped his thoughts from traveling too far down rabbit holes he didn't want to imagine. Looking at his wife, he saw desperation. He wanted to fix this. He wanted to fix his daughter, and I have no doubt he would have traded places with her at the snap of a finger if he could. Ultimately, he would not go down without a fight.

So, Jairus ran.

He had a destination, though he didn't know the exact location. His destination was not a place but a person. As he approached the market, he would hurriedly blurt out, "Where is He? I need to find Jesus!" Jairus knew time was not on his side and that finding Jesus was his last and only hope. The crowds were likely shoulder to shoulder. When Jesus was around, people knew. Everybody wanted to see what this Jesus guy was all about. Jairus found his way to where the crowds were starting to gather. Sure enough, there He was, near the beach after having just exited a boat.

When Jairus found Jesus, he fell at His feet, begging Him to come to his home and heal his daughter. He humbled himself at the feet of Jesus. He skipped the elaborate story about how his daughter's health had deteriorated and how they had tried everything humanly possible to help, but to no avail. No. Jairus got right to the point. "My little daughter is at the point of death, please come and lay Your hands on her so that she will get well and live" (Mark 5:23). Jairus spoke with confidence and desperation. He knew Jesus could heal his daughter, but the final move was up to Jesus.

Jairus did what he needed to do as a dad. It didn't matter to him what others would think of him. He was a synagogue official, and going to Jesus would have placed him in a unique position. He was a leader tasked with overseeing the worship, teaching, and all that would go on at the synagogue. Many in his position were at odds with Jesus. In Luke 13:14, we read about another synagogue official who challenged Jesus' healing work on the Sabbath. This official was so upset with Jesus that he called Him out in front of a crowd in his synagogue. It was his responsibility to protect the laws he was accustomed to.

Jairus, however, in a moment of desperation, felt his responsibility was to heal his daughter. And he knew Jesus was the only One who could do just that. At the risk of putting a target on his back for aligning with Jesus, Jairus did what he needed to do.

I asked my wife, Tiffani, to read through the passages in Matthew, Mark, and Luke's Gospels detailing this story and tell me what she thought Jairus' wife might have been doing during this crisis. "I'm sure she stayed with her daughter," she said. "The Mom would stay with her daughter so she wouldn't have to be alone. I would tell you to go get Jesus—go get the doctor. I'm staying with my kid."

These are the roles we play as parents. Her response was lived out during our beach trip in the hospital with Lily. Tiffani wasn't going to leave her side. I pressed a little further, asking, "Why would you say it's my role to go and yours to stay with our daughter?" Her reply was simple. "Because I wouldn't leave her—a Mom isn't going to leave her kid's side if she doesn't have to."

So, Jairus' wife stayed by her daughter's side. Most likely, she held her, comforted her, talked with her, sang to her, stroked her hair, rubbed her back, and prayed for her. It's what moms do. Jairus ran to Jesus. It's what dads do. We have different roles to play.

SHIFITING ROLES

What roles do you play within your home and marriage? Some of the roles we play are purposefully laid out and agreed on. Some happen because of how each person was raised and simply lived out after marriage. Some roles fit. Others don't. Some roles shift over the years.

CENTERING JESUS

When we're at our best, we can play off our individual strengths to divide roles within a marriage. Tiffani and I walk through premarital counseling with engaged couples, and this is an area that gets a solid chunk of time. Two individuals coming together with different strengths and weaknesses need to learn how to navigate those together. One particular area that seems to get this conversation started revolves around finances. When we ask, "How will the two of you handle finances and budgeting?" we are often hit with a couple of shrugs. Finances have the potential to cause a lot of stress in a marriage, but determining who will do what from the start—or a fresh start for couples who have been together for years—helps to ease that potential strain. "Who is good with finances and likes to handle budgeting?" This one tends to get mixed results. One of three answers is given: both, neither, or one distinct partner. No matter the answer, it starts us down a path of helping the couple determine the role each will play in handling finances. The most important aspect is that couples engage in the conversation around roles and responsibilities so that they are on the same page. This conversation often leads to how the couple will handle other aspects of their marriage—household chores, planning the family calendar and, when applicable, roles to play when parenting.

Our roles continue to need refining and redefinition as our kids continue to grow. I'm a guy with five daughters and no sons. I'm swimming in a house of females, which means I'm willing to shake the norms when it's called for.

Brinley needed a bra. So, I took her to a couple stores in town. Walking into one, we started looking for signs that would direct us when one of the associates met us and asked, "Is there something I can help you find?" I responded by asking if she could direct us to the bra section—not a question I had asked up to this point. The associate looked directly at Brinley and said, "Oh, I'm sorry you have to go shopping with Dad for this!" After shooting a quick look of disapproval toward my daughter, we walked in the direction the attendant pointed. "I'm not a fan of how she said that. I think it's wrong to send the message that we can't shop together simply because you need a bra. I certainly won't have the insight your mom would have, but I would assume that's what the people who work here are around to help with if we need it." After all, what if I had been a single dad trying to play the role of dad and mom? I would hope someone would encourage that dad along his journey and not put up more barriers. It was a good reminder to encourage one another in the roles we play as parents, whatever those roles may be.

There are times and seasons of life, whether married or single, that we may have to take on roles that weren't previously ours or that are simply shifting due to life circumstances. Jobs change, health changes, and even our individual strengths and weaknesses can evolve. Which means that flexibility and communication are key to long-term success. Knowing the roles we are to play and talking through them will set the stage for greater joy and understanding through all the tests and trials.

MARRIAGE VS. KIDS

As their daughter's life was slipping away, Jairus and his wife were absolutely focused on her. Their lives increasingly revolved around coming up with treatment plans and talking to anyone who could help or simply offer suggestions. When I put myself in their shoes, I can imagine that their conversations were consumed by their daughter and her health. They would have had tunnel vision during this time, and it would have not only been acceptable but necessary and appropriate.

As their daughter regained her health and their lives transitioned back to a normal schedule, I assume their conversations and daily plans no longer revolved around their daughter. Again, if I were in their shoes, it seems likely that they would continue in the roles they had prior to the health scare. That they would regain the marital rhythm they had lost during the battle for their little girl's health.

If it sounds like I'm suggesting that marriages are more important than kids, well, it's because I am.

The relationship we have with our spouse is more important than the relationship we have with our kids. Some of you may be wondering what you're still doing reading this book. I get it. This is a tough statement. It is an even tougher statement to live out.

Our kids need us. They rely on us. It is our job to keep them alive. From little on, we are figuring out how to navigate this world with someone who is now our responsibility. Especially when they are young, it is our responsibility to nurture, feed, clothe, cuddle, and foster a relationship that will last a lifetime. They are fully dependent on us. They need us.

Our kids also need us to demonstrate a healthy marriage. A healthy marriage puts the marriage before the kids. If our marriage is unhealthy, it will trickle down to our kids, and you can guarantee that they will feel it. You may be reading this from the vantage point of having gone through a tough relationship, or maybe you're single or living in a blended family. No matter where you are right now, you can choose to put your spouse before your kids.

What does it mean to put your spouse before your kids? Put the time in to be unified.

Our goal is to be a united team in parenting. In order to do that, we have to put the time in—together. Our kids will naturally consume a lot of our time, but that cannot mean that we do so at the cost of sacrificing too much time with our spouse. During these parenting years, we can be purposeful and intentional in scheduling time together. We need time together for different reasons and in different seasons. We need both daily and extended time together to continue to foster a deeper, unified relationship.

A general rule of thumb is to schedule daily time together to debrief on the day, talk over schedules, and make sure the logistics of the home and all activities are being handled.

Weekly dates are valuable for having time away from kids to be able to connect relationally and talk through any further issues that come up in our parenting. These weekly dates can be a regularly scheduled date night where you get a babysitter or they can be some sort of time slot during the week where kids are at school, asleep, or are involved in activities where you can have a focused conversation.

Monthly, schedule a half day or day together.

Quarterly, get away for a night.

Yearly, spend a week on vacation together—just the two of you.

Now, I realize there will be many different reactions to this sequence of one-on-one time together. For some, it may seem like an unattainable ideal, that finding someone to watch your kids in this season doesn't seem like an option. Or maybe you think it would simply tug too much at your mommy or daddy heartstrings to leave your kids for an extended period of time. Let me suggest that the cost of babysitters and trips away, to whatever degree you are able in this season of life, is worth the price of a solid marriage. The emotional challenge of being away from our children is worth the value added to the lifelong investment that is our relationship with our spouse. In order to be a unified couple, we need to choose to put the time into our relationship. And you know what? The outcome is a Christ-centered, unified blessing to our kids.

What do I mean when I say unified marriage? It means we can enter into anything as a united front. Our kids challenge us—daily. We are constantly making decisions about what to allow and what to put a stop to. What to say yes to and what to say no to. Our desire is to parent on purpose and not by accident. We want to be proactive rather than reactive.

When Tiffani and I spend time together, we talk through the issues that are currently coming up and those we anticipate will come up. We get on the same page so that way when our kids come up to either of us, we have a confident, united answer. If we don't have a confident answer, we can easily defer until we have time to talk it over. Then, when our kids push back on an answer, the other spouse can join the party by supporting what the other has already said. Over time, our girls have learned they can't play us because we always have the same answer. Which brings me to a key question, "What happens when one of us gives an answer the other person wouldn't support?" Before arguing ensues, we talk about it in private, get on the same page, then share our unified answer. If the final decision has changed as a result of us getting on the same page, well, we simply let them know we have talked more about it and come to a final conclusion that aligns closer to our values. Sure, there's a chance the kids will be disappointed or even upset about the change. Either way, unity is our projected front.

In the same way that we enter into daily challenges united, we enter into health scares united as well. I picture Jairus and his wife functioning like a team. I imagine them putting time into their relationship so when the crisis struck and stress washed over their home, they were able to lean on one another. They could be strong where challenges have the potential to weaken and divide. I picture this because I have been down the sick child road a couple times. I imagine Jairus handling his situation the way I do because I have been there. Tiffani and I were not divided by Lily's diabetes diagnosis but leaned on one another as we figured it out together. We played different roles, but we played them together.

It's like that old adage of a struggling married couple saying, "Hey, let's have a child. That'll bring us together!" I hate to be the bearer of bad news, but having kids will not bring a couple closer together. Quite the opposite, it will reveal the weaknesses of the marriage as if under a microscope. No matter whether we are new parents or seasoned vets, we need to be united within our marriages. We need to place our spouse above our kids in the order of how we prioritize our lives. Spend time together— daily, weekly, monthly, quarterly, and yearly. Work on our communication. Attend marriage retreats. Read books together. Pray together. I need it. You need it. Our kids need it.

THE ROLE WE PLAY IN THEIR MARRIAGE

Dads, who do you want your daughters to marry? Be that man.

Moms, who do you want your sons to marry? Be that woman.

We are raising our children to understand what a healthy marriage is intended to be like. If we want our kids to grow up to marry someone and live in a healthy marriage, we are setting that standard for them. If we want them to invest in a unified and healthy marriage, then we can model that for them today.

The way we treat our spouse will be the way our kids not only expect to be treated but how they will likely treat their own spouse. We set that standard. If our goal is for our children to marry individuals who treat them with love, compassion, kindness, humility, patience, and any other words we might use to describe their future spouse, then we need to be that person to our spouse.

The way we handle conflict, conversations, and struggles in our marriage are things our kids will witness and replicate when they are in a marriage. Like it or not, they will grow up believing how we handle things is normal—whether healthy or not. Not only should we work on our marriage to have a better one today for our sake, but we also want to model it so that our kids strive for a healthy marriage when they're at that stage in life.

Think of your marriage today. Are there things you do automatically that you can look back and realize it is because your parents did the same thing?

Along the same line of thinking, how we treat our kids is also an indicator of the person they will look to marry. I believe parents of the opposite gender have an impact on the expectations our kids will have when they look for a significant other. In other words, dads, you and I will impact the image our daughters hold of the man they will want to spend their lives with. Likewise, moms, your sons will view their future wives through the picture of womanhood that you display.

I have heard this story about how the government trains its fraud department to spot counterfeit money. It would be reasonable to think they study all sorts of counterfeits so they can understand what fake money may look like and spot a variety of counterfeits when they see them. However, as the story goes, this is not how they train their department. Instead, they study real money. They study it so intently that anything that's not real stands out. They know authentic money so well that counterfeits stand out anytime they look at, touch, or examine it. As parents, we want to be the real thing. We want to be so real that anything that doesn't seem to be in line with our healthy display of marriage will be spotted as counterfeit.

Dads, date your daughters. Moms, date your sons. Court them. Love them. Treat them well. In chapter two, when noting that we schedule what's important, I shared about the rotating schedule posted in our kitchen with a "who is next up" list for our daddy-daughter dates. It isn't just that these dates are important to me and my schedule, but that they get to see and feel the love I have for them on these dates. They are absorbing this information whether they realize it or not. They are starting to take in how I treat them, talk with them, and ask them questions. They witness how I treat our waiters and waitresses, the people we meet in the restaurants, and they are starting to form an impression about how a guy should treat them and other people. I know that I am setting a standard, for better or worse, about how they will expect to be treated and the character of the person they may date in the future.

I want to love my girls with a pure, unconditional kind of love so obviously that when they are looking for a husband, they will spot anything that feels off—they will spot the counterfeit. This is a high calling. This is intimidating. This is their future in our hands. We can embrace it with God's help as we seek to love them the way He loves us. Of course, we will not be perfect. I get the sense our kids already know that about us. But how we handle our imperfections will also indicate the type of love we have for them. A real love.

THE ROLE WE CAN'T OFFLOAD

Over the past couple of decades, there has been an increasing focus on children's and youth ministries in churches. Churches striving to provide effective, engaging, and interactive ministries to children up through their high school years. Let me start by stating that I am an absolute advocate of children's and youth ministries. I love the children's ministry at our church. My kids love their teachers and friends, and they hear about Jesus on a weekly basis. What's there not to like? I am also a huge advocate of youth ministry. I was a Youth Pastor for seven years, and I love what we are able to do by bringing teens together to help build relationships with Jesus, their adult leaders, and other teens. These ministries can have a significant impact on our kids. They had, and continue to have, a significant impact on each of my daughters.

The downfall to these largely successful ministries is that they can give us, parents, the idea that teaching our kids about Jesus is the church's role. That simply is not the case. It is absolutely our role to be the primary disciple-makers in our homes. We cannot delegate that duty to the church leaders. We cannot offload the responsibility of teaching our kids about Jesus to the "professionals." I believe it is the church's role to come alongside, support, and reinforce what is already happening at home. The local church can support what we do at home with the hour or two they have with our kiddos, but what we model and teach at home the rest of the week will have a greater impact. Their foundational beliefs will be rooted in what they grow up watching and hearing at home.

So, how do we foster their spiritual growth in our home? Part of it is organic. It's how we live. We model for our kids what a walk with Jesus looks like every day. How we live our lives is the greatest teacher to our kids of what Christianity looks like. It's why discerning and living out Christ-centered values is so vital. They see what we do, how we talk, and how we live in light of our faith.

Do our kids see our faith in action?

Do they see us reading our bibles?

Do they see us praying to rejoice as well as in times of need?

Do they hear us making decisions based on what God's Word says?

When we live our lives out in faith, we organically point our kids to Christ and to a growing relationship with Him.

In the same way that we regularly attend a church service, part of leading our kids to walk with the Lord can also be structured. We can strategically plan how to help foster our kids' relationship with Jesus. Throughout the years, we have put different plans into place. We have gone through children's bible stories, daily devotionals, and other materials during our nightly prayer time with our kids. Consistency is helpful. Establishing spiritual disciplines at early ages and stages can help foster healthy habits well into adulthood.

Recently, I invited my family to participate in a daily Bible reading plan with me. I had copies of a bible reading plan that would start with the first chunk of Genesis and then go through the New Testament. The plan went through a chapter or two each day and seemed like a reasonable goal for my kids between nine and fifteen years old to accomplish. I did not want to mandate it, but I hoped they would jump in with me. I suggested we do it together, and since we would all be reading the same thing at the same time, we could talk through questions we may have together. Four of my five kids, along with my wife, took on the challenge, each creating a plan on when they would try to read each day. We were all eager to start. A couple have found they enjoy hearing it read to them while they follow along. A couple have gone back and forth between reading in the mornings before they do anything else and reading after school or even later into the night. Sometimes, I even find them reading during our commute to or from school. Whatever the case, they are each working out their plans for themselves. Sure, I have talked with them throughout and encouraged them to determine what works for them. And yes, I have had to give reminders from time to time. But for the most part, it has largely been up to them. In this challenge, I believe it is my role to offer the invitation to join me and to model it along the way as I actively teach them about the spiritual discipline of reading their Bibles.

Personally, I am a fan of organized and structured spiritual disciplines. They keep us grounded and growing. Helping our kids find the benefits of a grounded and growing relationship with Jesus can be nurtured through organized spiritual disciplines. The only catch is, if we organize it for our kids without living it personally, you know, the do as I say, not as I do approach, be prepared for some fallout.

CONCLUSION

Before I add a little pressure, if you're a dad and have read up to this point, you need to give yourself some credit. Just by reading this, you have demonstrated that you are willing to put the time and effort into learning and growing, and that shows you care about your kids and your family. You want to raise them well. You're looking for support, suggestions, and ways to keep the ball moving forward. Great job!

So, dad, let me put a little added pressure on. I believe the family goes as we go. Any quick online search about fatherhood will reveal the impact a father has in the home, for good or bad. Fatherlessness has huge negative implications for the lives of kids. On the flip side, a little online research will show that fathers who stick around and follow Christ have a positive impact on their kids' lives and faith. Watching families in church over the years, I have witnessed what happens when a dad is actively involved. Often, what I see is a family that follows his lead. The mom is involved in serving, and the kids are active in children's or youth ministry, serving alongside their parents. These families are units serving the Lord together. They are committed to their church family and live their lives centered on Jesus. Dads have an important role to play. If we lead the way, I believe our families will follow.

Of course, this section is not meant to downplay the role of mom. Without a doubt, we all know moms are the glue to our families and to our churches. Faithful moms who follow the Lord will play any role needed in order to have a Jesus-centered home. If you're a single mom or a mom who does not have a believing spouse, your role is more challenging but not fruitless. I have watched countless mothers lead their kids to know and love Jesus. I have watched faithful wives continue to love Jesus alongside their reluctant husbands. Husbands who, after years of prayer, finally follow her example and come to know our Savior. Moms who have a believing husband and dads with a believing wife have the privilege of doing life together, leading their kids with Jesus at the center of their home. Parents, we have such important roles to play in raising kids who love Jesus.

Over the years, I have had people come up to me and highlight some of the teens we have had in our youth group who have put their faith on display through serving and leading by example. When this happens, they often ask, "What are you doing to produce kids like this?" My response has not changed much over the years. "It has less to do with what we are doing and more to do with the name on the back of the jersey." When there is a name on the back of a jersey, it is usually the player's last name. Likewise, a student whose faith shines has more to do with the home that the student was raised in than anything we are doing. Of course, as a church, we are doing everything we can to help foster a growing relationship with Christ. Yet, when I see our "successful" students, much of the time, though certainly not always, I see kids who come from homes that are following Jesus wholeheartedly together.

We all have a role to play. Jairus played his role. His wife played hers. What is the role Jesus is asking you to play in your home today?

BRIAN SCHLEY

6 REFLECTION QUESTIONS

1. How would you describe the roles you play in your home? If married, what roles does your spouse play? How did you establish the roles each of you currently live out? Are there any roles that could be shifted?

2. Does your home currently reflect the idea that the marriage relationship requires a greater priority than the parent-child relationship?

3. What daily, weekly, monthly, and yearly one-on-one relationship rhythms do you and your spouse live out? How do you structure dedicated time together in order to strengthen your marriage?

4. If your child(ren) were to grow up to marry someone like you, what would you be excited about? What would you be concerned about?

5. We are the most prominent disciple-makers in our kids' lives. How are you currently discipling your children?

7 Do Not Fear Your Fear

"Oh, just wait until they are teenagers!" Countless times I have heard that line since my girls were little. The suggestion being that I should nervously anticipate the day they turn thirteen because, at that point, a switch would flip, turning my dream into a nightmare. Now, I understand that teenage years bring new challenges for our kids and for us as parents. Yet, should we count down the days, dreading the coming teen years?

Each season of our kids' lives holds challenges, just in different ways. Early on, they are solely dependent on us. We feed, change, clothe, comfort, rinse, lather, and repeat. Our job is caretaker. When they become mobile, we become defenders. We defend them from all things that can break them. And we defend those things that are in reach of being broken by them. We are "on" at all times, unable to let them out of our sight, aware that something destructive or devastating could happen at any moment.

As they continue to age, they become less dependent on us, slowly gaining and fighting for independence. We journey through this season by teaching, re-teaching, hovering, letting go, and watching from a short distance away as they learn to navigate the world around them. Once in their teens, they are discerning and developing their identity. They have a foundation and are wrestling with the world around them in new ways.

The good-hearted folks who warn us about the teen years certainly have some good reasons to throw caution our way. But considering that each phase of parenting has its unique challenges, I honestly find it hard to caution someone on which particular season to beware of.

I do know that if we go into any season of parenting fearful and anxious, we will struggle through it. If we are already dreading something, we will walk in, ready for it to be over as soon as possible. Rather, if we walk into each season as a new opportunity, we will get the most out of it. And you know what? So will our kids. These years go by fast enough, and I'd like to enjoy the journey. It is not healthy or helpful to fear any of the parenting years. We don't have to fear when we have Jesus on our side.

JAIRUS

No doubt, Jairus was fearful for his daughter and even for himself. Whether driven by fear, love, or some other force, Jairus ran in search of Jesus. And he was successful in convincing Jesus to return to see his daughter—to heal her. As the group began its journey to Jairus' home, they received word that the girl was not just dying but had, in fact, died while Jairus was away. Jesus, despite the news, continued walking. Rather than offer Jairus a prayer, something to eat, or an embrace, Jesus looked at him and said, "Do not be afraid any longer; only believe, and she will be made well" (Luke 8:50).

Jesus told Jairus not to fear.

There was nothing to fear if he simply believed, and Jairus had already demonstrated belief. It was the reason he found Jesus that morning. Jairus believed Jesus was the only one who could help his daughter. Now, with the most troubling news piercing his heart, Jairus would have been presented with a new fear—a new sense of despair. Yet, Jesus simply told him not to fear.

What should he do instead of fearing? It is not enough to tell someone not to do something. It's like saying, "Don't think of a pink elephant." The next thing we think about is a pink elephant before we even get to try not to think of a pink elephant. So, when Jesus told Jairus not to fear, the natural response was likely to think about all the things he should be afraid of at this point. Jesus knew this. Which is why he didn't leave Jairus to figure it out on his own. Instead, Jesus quickly followed up his statement, "Do not fear," with "believe."

Believe what? Believe in Jesus, and all will be well.

Still, Jesus went further in his brief message to Jairus, telling him what would happen if he believed—his daughter would be made well. She would be healed. In this case, she would not remain dead but would live.

Jesus doesn't want us to be fooled into thinking this world will be easy. If you're a parent, you certainly understand this already. Parenting is not for the weak. Parenting provides a seemingly endless series of opportunities for fear to rise up within us. Jesus told us we would face trials, tribulations, and struggles in this world—whether parenting or not (John 16:33). After letting us know not to expect the easy road, He followed up by telling us to live courageously because He had already overcome this world. He had defeated death. He defeated sin. He was and is victorious.

When we put our trust in Jesus we are trusting the One who reigns and rules over all, including me and my kids. Since we can trust in Him, we can live at peace through the inevitable struggles that will arise. Since we can trust in Him, we can live courageously through them all.

We have not been created to live in fear.

Fear cripples. Fear retreats. Fear mourns. Fear produces inaction.

Jairus hit a point where fear could cripple. Jesus, however, suggested a different approach—belief. Trust. Courage. In other words, Jesus was inviting Jairus to step into the current and future reality of parenting with peace and courage. And how did Jairus respond to this invitation? He continued on his journey home with Jesus only to find that what Jesus said did, in fact, happen. His precious little girl would be okay. There was never any need to fear. The need was to keep walking with Jesus, believe, and be courageous. Fear not.

FEAR OR TRUST

You and I, each and every day, can choose either to trust or to fear.

Fear is real. Fear is what I felt every time Sophie felt sick. Whenever she had a fever, fear struck. The first year of remission was the most daunting because it was the most likely time for her cancer to return. And while the likelihood of its return faded over time, the reminder was constantly there in those early years. So, anytime she got a little bug of some sort, or she popped even the slightest fever, fear that her cancer had returned rose up within me. It was a much different reaction than when my other girls got sick or came down with a fever. I didn't think much of it. After all, they go to school in a petri dish of germs and are likely to get something every now and then. Sophie, though swimming in the same petri dish, when she would get sick, it hit me differently.

We can choose to be struck by fear or to live our lives trusting Jesus. This was an ongoing reminder for me over the years. Each time Sophie would get sick, I would have to ask myself if I was going to allow the fear of her illness returning to consume me or if I was going to trust in God's plan. Over the years, it has gotten easier. As I write this, she has well passed the magical five-year mark of being cancer-free. That was a huge line to cross for all of us. When she gets sick now, fear is not my fall-back response. It is as if time has a way of changing old fears into new trusts. Each fever along the way was a test of my faith. I was tested on how I would choose to respond. Each was an opportunity to remember that God has not given me a spirit of fear but of love and courage and a deep trust in Him (2 Timothy 1:7).

The Bible talks frequently about our fears. Jesus gets it. He gets us. He doesn't want us to be crippled by fear because when we are, we aren't living our lives to the fullest. And this is important because we are all on a journey. We are on a parenting journey. And on this wild adventure, fear is not helpful. So, when we find ourselves relying on fear as our default, let's try and shift to live lives of trust one opportunity at a time.

BRIAN SCHLEY

DON'T BE AFRAID TO HAVE THE CONVERSATION

When in doubt, have the conversation. It doesn't matter what conversation topic we are talking about. In marriage, with kids, at work, in the neighborhood—when in doubt, have the conversation. What keeps us from having difficult conversations is usually fear. How is this going to turn out if I bring it up? Will talking about it make it worse? Will I say the right thing? Will they be mad at me? Usually, we build up the conversation and all the "what-ifs" to be way bigger and much worse than it often turns out to be in reality. Whatever the case, as a general rule of thumb, have the conversation.

As parents, we will be faced with many opportunities to ask questions, take on challenges, and lean into difficult conversations. Let's commit right now to having the difficult conversations as they arise. If we are wondering about what our kids' thoughts are on something, let's ask them. We may or may not get an answer, or we may not get an answer we like, but at least we are having the conversation.

Ignorance is not bliss when it comes to parenting. Sometimes, I'll hear parents say something like, "Yeah, I just don't want to know if he's actually doing that. If I don't know, then I can act like it's not going on." Maybe that sounds burden-free, with a blind hope that our kids may not be involved in something that could be against our values, but let's call it what it is—fear taking over. I'll often respond by saying, "If they're doing what you fear, then you should know. Either way, they're doing it, and if you know, at least you'll have the opportunity to walk through it with them." We can choose to consider it a blessing to know when our kids mess up. Why? Because if they mess up while under our roof, we have an opportunity to teach, shape, and mold them. When they mess up after moving out on their own, then our options as parents are limited.

If we make asking questions the norm in our homes, then it won't feel so awkward to us or our kids when we dig in a little deeper. Start early, ask often. We can regularly ask questions about their days, friendships, or activities that develop a normal baseline in asking questions. We can get more personal and ask about hygiene, puberty, and dreams. We can actually make asking these questions normal. Then, when something seems a bit off, they won't be surprised when we lean in and ask about it.

Normalize difficult conversations. Have challenging conversations, and have them openly. The birds and the bees talk doesn't need to be secretive and under some sort of mysterious coded language. Talking about alcohol or drugs shouldn't be ignored or kept in the dark, assuming that because they already know what's expected, they won't be tempted or need to discuss these things. If we start early and often, then we can have these conversations as if they are normal because they are.

The question frequently comes up about when to talk to our little ones about sex, drugs, and dating. My suggestion is earlier than you would like. And when you do, I would also suggest having them on an age-appropriate level. Use words, phrases, and examples that meet them where they're at. If your kids are involved in school or settings with many other kids, the likelihood that others are talking about these things is fairly high. So, if you suspect that your child may be wading into these more mature and challenging waters, your suspicion is probably accurate.

We have gone about it rather directly by asking a question like, "Hey, what have you heard about sex?" This way, we have a point of reference from which to give accurate information—at an age-appropriate level.

BRIAN SCHLEY

Another aspect of addressing these topics openly is that we want to be the first to have these types of conversations with our kids. We value laying the foundation, which means we err on the side of earlier rather than later. If they are starting to hear things, we want to begin the conversation with them to provide accurate information and to establish the ground rules that we can talk openly and honestly in our home about these topics. It's a struggle to know when the timing is right, but like I said earlier, if you're wondering if the time is now, then it probably is. But until that point, we usually tell our kids something like, "Hey, there are some things we just haven't told you about yet, but we will in the future." Yes, that mysterious comment usually comes with a little pushback, but we're okay with that. The goal is simply to let them know that we will reveal more information at a more age-appropriate time.

Tiffani and I don't want to be afraid to have difficult conversations with our kids. We know that for parents to confidently have them when they're teens it means we need to start when they're toddlers. We need to ask questions when things seem off. Ask questions when things seem normal. Lean into sticky situations. We need to normalize talking about challenging topics. Our kids will talk with someone when they have questions. If you're like me, you want them to feel comfortable talking with you as much as possible.

DON'T FEAR THE GUILT YOU FEEL

Mom-guilt is real. That's what my wife tells me. I'm not a Mom, but I do feel the guilt of "not measuring up." It can seem like we are treading water through these parenting years, just trying to get by without messing our kids up too much. Tiffani and I often say to Ashley, our oldest kiddo, that she's just trial and error. We've never parented anyone older than her before, so it's a bit of a learning curve for all of us. Yet, here we are, trying to figure things out just like you because, quite honestly, we don't have everything figured out. Not to mention, our kids are not an assembly line where the same thing works for each of them. It's because they aren't cookie cutouts of one another that we can quickly feel like we are failing at the parenting game.

When we feel we are failing as parents, guilt sets in. Guilt is a horrible feeling that tears us down to our core. It cripples us. It stunts our ability to make decisions. It harms our ability to parent. Guilt, as you can see, is not a tool God uses in our lives.

The technology-obsessed society we live in doesn't help matters. We are constantly connected to social media screaming at us that we don't measure up. Our friends, family, and strangers post online about all the parenting successes they have while we are buried beneath a dirty pile of "would haves" and "should haves" at home. We turn to social media to watch the amazing vacations, family outings, social events, perfectly manicured kids, travel team trophies, birthday party galas, all the newest toys, and all the other things that bring us to the point of feeling like we don't measure up.

Comparison kills.

That's what our world is offering us. The opportunity to feel like we don't measure up to all the "perfect" parents out there. We see and feel the guilt of our real and mostly imagined failures and shortcomings. We want what's best for our kids, yet we aren't offering what all others seem to be. We compare. We feel less than and thus guilty. It's mom-guilt. It's parent-guilt.

The reality is what we see is not reality. Or, at least, it's not the whole reality. We all post pictures and tell stories of our successes. Our vacations, our clean homes, our kids dressed up for an event, their achievements, and all other highlights we share with the world. Seldom do we post the meltdowns—theirs or ours—the messy house, the arguments, the losses, the long showers to pull it all back together. We compare our worst days with others' best days. It is not their whole reality, and it is not ours, either.

Even when we don't compare, we have an ideal picture of our lives and our kids' lives in our heads that we want to strive for. Guilt sets in quickly when our ideal is not met. We can feel like we are letting our kids, our spouse, and even God down. Guilt settles in deep too.

No doubt, Jairus could have been feeling guilty about his daughter's condition. He could have been thinking back to all the signs he had missed. Feeling guilty for not seeking help earlier. Questioning everything they had done or fed her over the past days, weeks, or months. He might have compared himself to the parents around him who didn't have a sick child. Or compared himself to the type of fathers he had hoped he would be.

It was in the middle of all of this potential worry that Jesus told him to stop worrying and to not be afraid, but instead, simply believe and trust in Him and who He made Jairus to be, particularly the father of that sick little girl. If we are feeling guilty, Jesus has instructed us to stop looking within and start looking up. Guilt, the sort that defeats us, does not come from God. Believe, hope, and trust do.

When we compare ourselves to others, we are looking out and in rather than up. We are looking at others. We are looking within ourselves. And we are viewing ourselves as someone who does not measure up outwardly or inwardly. The problem is that this prevents us from looking up to the One who has made us in His image. When we finally look up, we realize that we already have all we need to raise our kids in the love God has for us and in who He is continuing to form us into. As parents, we are not perfect. We can't be. There is only One to ever walk this planet who was—Jesus—and He is on our side. He wants to do this journey with us. He wants to remove all of the guilt we're hauling around. He wants us to look to Him as our guide rather than the social media that manipulates.

So, we give our guilt to God. We allow ourselves to feel the grace He has so graciously given us. Yes, we will have low points and mess up, but God's grace covers our mess-ups. Instead of feeling guilty, we feel grace. We walk confidently, not because of our abilities, but because of His. We move forward with lessons learned and leave the guilt behind. It hinders and holds us back rather than helping us step into the grace God has for us in our parenting. We don't have to fear the guilt we feel.

DON'T BE AFRAID TO APOLOGIZE

When we mess up, and we will mess up, we shouldn't be afraid to apologize to our kids. Many of us grew up believing or at least being told that parents are always right. Some of us grew up believing that apologizing is admitting failure or weakness. This couldn't be any further from the truth. Apologizing makes us stronger—parents and kids. Apologizing mends relationships. It brings about the notion that perfection is not normal, expected or attainable.

My kids have varying degrees of ability to apologize. Some

apologize freely. Some struggle to do so even when they know they're in the wrong. The words, "I'm sorry," seem to catch in their throat. Even harder for kids and adults, "Will you forgive me?" Yet, when we model apologizing to our kids, they warm up to the idea that it is a healthy and good response when our shortcomings temporarily take over.

Apologizing to our kids makes us normal.

Apologizing to our kids models to them what we should be doing when we make mistakes.

Apologizing is teaching them an appropriate response to handling mistakes.

It is healthy.

It is good.

It is modeling.

It is parenting.

DON'T BE AFRAID TO LEAD THE WAY

Leadership leads. Is that too simplistic? Leadership lets us all know where we are going. It centers our attention on a common goal. Teams are often focused on winning. It is a common bond that brings the team together. Whether on a team, at work, or in parenting, we seek leadership. As parents, you and I can lead our families toward a goal as well. We can point our kids toward the common bond we have together.

What we focus on gets the attention. What we tend to think about or worry about can consume us. If we are looking for reasons to be worried, we will find them. If we are looking for the bad in a person, we will find it. If we are looking for challenges in our lives, we will find them.

Paul gave us a way to deal with worry. Quite simply, he told us to turn it over to God. Let Him handle it. But Paul didn't stop there. He didn't just tell us to stop worrying and let God handle our anxiety. After he told us to give our worries to God, he instructed us to think about good things. Focus on things that are true, honorable, right, lovely, pure, commendable, or anything worthy of praise (Philippians 4:6-8). What we give our attention to will capture our minds and our focus.

In our home, we focus on three things: show love, give grace, and share Jesus. Those are the three things we want to give our attention to. Tiffani and I attended a marriage retreat years ago that challenged us to write a family mission statement. We utilized Scripture that we valued, talked through a few questions they had given us to work through, and after a process, came up with our family mission statement: show love, give grace, and share Jesus.

Our family mission statement is not particularly unique, but it is ours. In a world where we can so quickly and easily focus on the negative aspects of life, our statement allows us to focus on the good things God offers us. After picking up the kids from school or during dinner together, we have the opportunity to ask each person in our family, kids and parents, to share how they showed love that day. Some days, it seems easy, and people are able to roll off a few examples within seconds. Other days, it is a struggle to come up with a single way someone demonstrated love to another person. The thing is, when we are consistent with asking this question, it becomes easier to answer as it becomes a regular part of each person's daily thought process. When we are focused on showing love to people during the day, it tends to come more naturally. One of the axioms we say when dropping our kids off at school is, "Go show love today!" We want to show love through action, letting our faith pour out of us.

How incredible would it be if we were so focused on this that it naturally spilled over? But as Tiffani and I witness within the walls of our home, we are in need of constant reminders to love one another within our family. Our family mission is not simply for those outside the walls of our home but right here, starting beneath our roof. Yeah, we have a long way to go, but we are focused. And we certainly have opportunities each day to discuss giving and receiving grace and what it means to share Jesus with other people. Each of these areas, we believe, is a good thing to focus on. And like Paul said, focusing our attention on good things can limit the worries that often overcome us.

Having developed a family mission statement has helped us focus our minds and our hearts on what we believe is true and right. We have it posted in our house in multiple areas. It's on a board in our living room, surrounded by family photos. It's also written in large letters at the top of the chalkboard wall in our kitchen. Yes, our kitchen wall has been painted with chalkboard paint. We write over every inch of it too. It has a large family calendar on it that gets updated regularly, like with daddy-daughter dates, our family prayer requests, current Bible reading plan and the chapters for that week, and even the amount of money we owe our kids from offering up chores. You know, the important stuff. And above it all is our family mission statement. Whenever we eat a meal at the table, the mission is above our heads. When we walk in the door, it's the first thing we see. It has given us a common language, a foundation from which we can talk. It points us to where we want to go and who we want to be.

CENTERING 🏠 JESUS

Each one of us has the opportunity to create a family mission statement. There are no rules. No age or time limits. Tiffani and I did ours without our kids because we were without our kids at a marriage retreat. When we came home, we met with our young girls at the time and shared with them what we came up with and what each area meant. If we were to do one now, I'm sure we would include the kids in it. We may tweak, change, or create a new one someday, but as of now, it still works and still needs to be worked on.

If you want to create a family mission statement, here's a little tip: start with the life verses you hold near and dear. Which Scripture passages resonate with you? What themes has God pressed into you time and again? How has He wired your family and brought you together to serve Him?

We all have some verses that we seem to cling to, or that seem to shape and guide our thinking. I can look at my kids, and different verses seem to stand out for each one. I believe God has wired them with longings and passions already at work in their hearts. What are we passionate about? What breaks our hearts? What motivates us to get up in the morning? What would cause us to uproot our lives and follow Him to be and do?

For my wife and I, James 1:22 still hits home. We want to be doers of the Word and not just hearers of it. We want to live lives that put God's Word into action. For us, that translated to "show love." We want to demonstrate the love that God asks of us. We are to love God and love people—the Great Commandment (Matthew 22:36-40). We want to live out what God's Word states.

Because of His love, we know that it is by grace we have been saved (Ephesians 2:8-9). When we feel that grace, we want others to feel it from us as a result. For us, that translates to "give grace."

This love and grace we have felt and want to share is the overflow of what Jesus has done for us. And we don't want to keep that to ourselves. We want to tell others about Jesus—the Great Commission (Matthew 28:18-20). For us, as a family unit, we want to "share Jesus."

When we have mission statements in our homes, we're setting our family up to be driven by what we are striving for and not by fear. Fear is a motivator, but not as great of a motivator as love. Fear does not come from the Lord. Love does.

We either run towards something in life, or we run away from something. When people talk to me about making changes in their lives, I often start by asking, "Are you running from something or toward something?" If we are running towards something God is leading us to, that's a good thing. If we are running from something that is currently frustrating, upsetting, difficult, etc., we may be motivated by something other than God's leading in our lives.

You are probably aware that life tends to get a bit crazy from time to time. When it does, a mission statement can ground us. When I'm counseling individuals who feel their life is in chaos, I'll often try to bring it back to a simple perspective like the Great Commission—love God, love people. So, when the fear takes root when they are presented with decisions that need to be made, relational challenges, career issues, or life seems to be out of control, and they don't know what to do, I try to bring them back to the basics and ask, "How are you doing at loving God and loving people right now?" If we can focus on those two aspects, many other things tend to fall into place. When we have something we are pursuing, like a mission, goal, or dream, the important things sort themselves out. Why? Because we know our values. We know what and Who we are chasing.

We all have some sort of mission we follow within our homes. Some are defined, some are not. For those of you who don't currently have a mission statement, you are still chasing something or, I suppose, running from something. Ask the others living in your home, "What would you say our family mission is?" You may be surprised at the answers you receive. If there are multiple people in your home, there's a good chance you will receive multiple perspectives. Having a family mission statement can bring clarity, purpose, and a common language to share with one another. It is a way to lead our families, not with fear but purpose.

LOVE THEM FEARLESSLY

We arrived home from China with a gift from a friend. She is an artist who painted a picture that read, "Love Her Fearlessly." What a perfect gift! We needed to see that. We needed to preach that to ourselves on a daily basis in those early days. Not because we didn't already love her deeply but because we were certainly fearful. We were afraid to go to doctor appointments and hear, "The cancer came back." As those early days turned to weeks and months, the fears slowed down but did not stop entirely. However, over time, as we continued to go in for check-ups, receiving positive news, the fear would ease ever so slightly. As years rolled by, when she would get sick, fear that the cancer had returned diminished. But the call to love her fearlessly remained vital, reminding us that we could not withhold our love out of the fear of potentially having to let go. We could not hold back pieces of our hearts just in case the cancer returned and we had to release her to be with Jesus. We needed to be able to push through our fear directly into love. Love casts out fear (1 John 4:18).

To this day, that painting still rests on the headboard in our bedroom. "Love Her Fearlessly." Its meaning has broadened. We may not be as fearful of the cancer returning as we were in those early days, but fear is certainly part of parenting. It is a part that I don't like, but it's there. "What if I mess up? What if I say the wrong thing? What if we treat them differently? What if they don't succeed?" The what-if game is one we will never win. Why? Because we will never have all the answers, perfect actions, or right decisions. What we can do, however, is choose to not succumb to parenting out of fear. We cannot be fearful of loving our kids. Rather, in the face of fear, we love. In the face of unknowns, we parent with confidence, not because of our own wisdom and power, but because of His.

The fears we faced with cancer have receded, but the temptation to fear has never changed. Whether one month, one year, or five years cancer-free, fear will never benefit us on this journey. God was and is with us through it all. It is His plan, isn't it? We just get the honor of being part of it.

The Bible frequently reminds us to not be fearful.

Do you know who needs to be encouraged to not be afraid? People who are afraid, that's who. God knows us. He knows we have fears. Each and every one of us. He also knows He is on our side and that we have nothing to fear. I get it. Easier said than done. Been there, done that. Yet, as He continues to be faithful, we can continue to let go of fear and hold onto Him.

When we do, we can love them fearlessly.

7 REFLECTION QUESTIONS

1. How much does fear impact your life and parenting? Name the fears that grip you as a parent. How can you release the fear that is not from God?

2. Do you connect with the story of Jairus? If so, how? He had reason to be afraid, yet Jesus told him to simply believe. What do you suppose Jesus would say to you in your context? What might Christians today learn from Jesus' interaction with Jairus?

3. How do fear and trust relate to one another? Does your level of trust in God influence the level of fear you live with? What can we do to grow our trust in God?

4. When debating whether to have a conversation, the general rule of thumb is to go ahead and have it. What keeps you from having what you perceive to be difficult conversations? How will you move past your fear in order to normalize deep or difficult conversations with your kids?

5. Having a family mission statement can help guide our families toward a unified goal and keep us grounded in our values and beliefs. Ask yourself, what Scriptures are anchors to your faith? What has God made you passionate about? If married, what has God uniquely brought the two of you together to do and be about? Take some time to discuss, pray about, and write out a family mission statement.

CENTERING JESUS

Centering on Jesus

"What is God trying to teach you this week?" I asked this of my girls during our family mission trip to Panama. "He's teaching me to listen to Him and respond according to what He wants for my life," said one of them. "Appreciation," said another. "I need to be more appreciative of what I have." The smile grew across my face as I silently gave thanks for what Jesus was doing in their hearts. It's the little things that become big things. These little comments keep me going. These little wins help me endure the struggles and trials of parenting. They keep me focused on chasing Jesus and putting Him at the center of our home.

Although the bible does not follow Jairus' life after He brought Jesus to his home, I wonder about the impact that day had on his family. After watching Jesus raise his daughter from dead to alive I have to believe Jairus would have been all-in as a disciple from that moment onward. And what about Jairus' wife? She had been with her daughter during her last breaths and then a witness to the miracle of her little girl wide awake and aware. And, of course, his daughter who most likely knew that she was withering away only to jump up and grab a bite to eat after Jesus' visit.

That type of impact continues for a lifetime. Generations even.

It's not always easy to see or navigate, and it is not always pretty, but it is worth it. Day in and day out Tiffani and I continue trying, desperately, to center our home on Jesus. I long for my kids to know and love Jesus. That's my prayer. My job is to help them know and love Him. So, as often as possible, we try to make decisions that do just that. We want to run our household based on biblical principles. We want Jesus to be at the center of our decision-making and in the center of our family.

If you've read this far, my guess is you also have a similar desire.

I need steady reminders that my goal is different from the goals the world sets out for me. When I am reminded that our time on this earth is limited, I am able to put into a proper perspective, an eternal perspective, what my ambitions are as a parent. It starts with me. It starts with us. We want to be the people our kids look up to and follow. They will, anyway—at least for a season. For that reason, we want to model who Jesus is, not requiring perfection but earnestly seeking after Him. When we seek after Him, we are able to trust Him more and more with our kids. After all, they are His and we are just borrowing them for a time. He entrusts them to us as stewards. So, we ought to trust Him.

As gatekeepers, we put boundaries around what and who comes into our kids' lives. When we parent differently than the world—when we parent according to the Bible—we will face adversity, not only from others but also from our kids. Dare to live differently. Parenting from a biblical foundation means that we have key roles to play within our home. God has a role, and He assigns us roles to play, along with those trusted individuals surrounding our kids' lives. When we play the role God has given us, we get to be the influence we need to be with the time we have.

None of this is easy. It is hard, demanding, and relentless, but worth it. We don't need to fear the challenges that we face as parents. Why? Because we have God, our Father, walking this journey with us. The ultimate parent guiding us in our parenting.

If you're new to this idea of biblical parenting, then let me just encourage you to start small. Start with something you may have gleaned from these pages and try to implement it into your home. Just one thing, not everything. Change is difficult, but by introducing one new thing and being consistent, that small change will lead to more little changes. Over time, little changes become big shifts in a home. Your small change may be praying before meals. Or just focusing on having family meals together. It could be putting phones down and playing a family game.

As you set out putting these things into practice, pray for your kids. Pray with your kids. Pray with your spouse. Start small and gain momentum. Little changes lead to big shifts.

A quick caution though before you dive in. Don't succumb to paralysis by analysis. If you're like me, you can analyze a change so much that it causes you to do nothing. We're paralyzed from overanalyzing our options. Here's the catch, doing something is better than doing nothing. So, take one step toward Jesus. One step in the direction you want to lead your family. You can continue to make changes along the way, but keep chasing Jesus and putting Him in the center of your home. It is worth it. It is worth it now. And it will be worth it for eternity.

Once you've come up with a goal, do some of the following

things to help you be successful.

Write it down.

Put that note somewhere to serve as a reminder.

Schedule it in your calendar or set up automatic reminders to help you stay on track.

Tell someone.

If you're married, talk it through with your spouse. Be on the same page. We are much more likely to stick to our plans and accomplish our goals when we tell others.

And let's just get this out in the open here and now—don't expect instant success.

When our kids are little, it is quite challenging to get them to sit still together as we read through a bible story or attempt to pray together as a family. But be patient. When you try something and it is challenging, that doesn't mean you shouldn't stick with it. It may pay off in the future as you establish healthy spiritual habits. At the same time, we want to consider how to best meet our kids where they're at. Reading children's bible stories with lots of pictures is great for younger children. Likewise, keeping prayers quick and simple, such as going around with each sharing one thing they're thankful for. Age appropriate actions are great building blocks. Again, be patient. We have to keep our hearts from getting discouraged during younger years or frustrated during the grumblings of later years. We are after lifelong habits which require nurturing to build.

Whether you're just starting this journey of putting Jesus at the center of your home or considering how to continue into the next season, I applaud you. Tiffani and I are right there with you. We're trying to figure it out one day at a time. Deep down, I want Jesus to be at the center of our home and all we do. So, let's press on. Let's endure. Let's encourage one another on this journey. It is not easy, but it is worth it.

BRIAN SCHLEY is a follower of Jesus, husband, father, pastor, and author. As a school counselor for nine years, Brian enjoyed working with children and parents while personally studying parenting. Upon transitioning into ministry, two passions merged, his biblical studies and his studies in parenting. Today, his master's degrees in counseling and ministry inform both his writing and speaking. Brian serves as a pastor, is co-host of the *Stand Up Radio Ministry* at standuppodcast.com, and offers pastoral coaching at Plethos Global. Brian lives in the countryside of Manitowoc, WI with his wife and five daughters.

www.ingramcontent.com/pod-product-compliance
Lightning Source LLC
Chambersburg PA
CBHW020359130626
46549CB00006B/2347